GOOD
BEER
GUIDE
TO
NEW
YORK

*Where to
Find and Drink
Good Beer
in New York*

by Timothy Harper
Foreword by
Michael Jackson

RUNNING PRESS
PHILADELPHIA · LONDON

About the Author

Timothy Harper is a journalist, lawyer, lecturer, travel writer, corporate communications consultant, international trade advisor and beer drinker – not necessarily in that order. A native of Peoria, Ill., who lived in Manhattan for several years before spending several more years in Europe, he now lives across the Hudson River in Ridgewood, N.J., with his wife, Nancy Bobrowitz, and their children, Lizzie and Jonathan. A frequent contributor to magazines and newspapers on both sides of the Atlantic, he is also the author of *Cracking the New European Markets*, and has written, edited and co-authored a number of other business and travel books.

9 8 7 6 5 4 3 2 1
Digit on the right indicates the number of this printing.
ISBN 1-56138-722-3

Cover and interior design by Milton Glaser
Maps by Tony Millionaire
Editorial, layout and production by Brown Packaging
Printed in Italy by Vincenzo Bona

This book may be ordered by mail from the publisher.
Please add $2.50 for postage and handling.
But try your bookstore first!

Running Press Book Publishers
125 South Twenty-second Street
Philadelphia, Pennsylvania 19103-4399

Contents

FOREWORD

By Michael Jackson

Good beer is enjoying a renaissance, but the majority of bars and restaurants still have not realized this. Perhaps they never will; after all, not every dining place serves good food.

Just as a devotee of the grape would not eat in a restaurant with a limp wine list, the beer lover has trouble going to a place with no decent brews – however much he or she might enjoy the ambiance, the company or the food.

Until recently, only a handful of places in New York offered good selections of beer. That has changed dramatically.

I long have had six or seven favorite spots in Manhattan, and one or two in Brooklyn, but that hardly covers the corners of New York where I might find myself within reach of a good pint...or the desires that might strike me. What I needed, and now have, is a guide that stretches from Williamsburg to Westchester. Where can I find a good beer with bagels and lox, or with mussels and fries? Where can I enjoy a great beer while my friend soothes herself with herbal tea? Where can I have a pensive pint with poetry or jazz? Which is the sexiest place to serve great beer? Where can I take my lover...or my kid?

Very occasionally, I am tempted into a famous bar that I know does not serve great beers. Perhaps the ambiance, or the conversation, will compensate? It never does; the experience is incomplete. That is why some famous New York bars are conspicuously absent from this guide. These days, plenty of good beers are available. A bar that does not stock a decent selection is too lazy to be worth visiting.

For lovers of characterful beers, New York was once a disappointment; now it is a delight. Many of the best products from microbreweries across America are here, and so are several of the quirkiest from beer lands like Britain, Belgium and Bavaria. What brought about this

4

metamorphosis? I like to think I encouraged it – but someone had to make the beers available, and it was the people at the Craft Brewers Guild who waved the wand. Their effort to promote and distribute the best beers from around the world was a stroke of genius. I thank them for the magical transformation.

What is good beer?

A good beer does more than quench the thirst. It rewards and soothes. It is a social lubricant. It arouses the senses and often the appetite. Some beers go well with certain foods. Some dishes are better accompanied by beer than by wine.

Good beer has taste. It also has aroma, length and finish. "No aftertaste" is adspeak for *bibendus interruptus*. Good beer tastes of the grains from which it was made: sometimes wheat, always malted barley, and occasionally oats or rye, for example. Those often-sweet flavors are balanced by the dryness of hop flowers. In a good lager, the flavors are distinctively clean. In a true ale, they are given more complexity and at least a hint of fruitiness by the type of yeast used. Good porters and stouts have the flavors of dark chocolate and espresso. Good wheat beers are tart and wonderfully refreshing.

A good beer invites another sip, and then a third. Each time, new aromas and flavors express themselves. When I sit quietly with a good beer, I am having an inner conversation with it: "Delicious maltiness...arousing hop flavor...a wry note of bitterness."

Anyone can do this. You don't have to be an expert, or crazy. All you need is a sense of smell and taste, just like any other human being. You also need a good beer. Here's where to find it...

Michael Jackson has been described by the *Wall Street Journal* as "the world's leading beer critic." His books include *The Simon and Schuster Pocket Guide to Beer, Michael Jackson's Beer Companion*, and *Great Beers of America*.

Introduction

Among the hundreds of bars and stores consid-
ered for this guide, several dozen were recommended by friends and acquaintances. One guy
with a twisted sense of humor – I can only
assume it was a guy – left me an unsigned note
insisting on a visit to the Pussycat Lounge in
Manhattan. A few days later, I walked into the
Pussycat as two nearly nude women strutted
through their routines on the bar. The bartender
leaned forward, cleavage heaving in her tiny red
elf's costume. (It was just before Christmas.)
"What kind of beer do you have?" I asked.

She blinked, and recited the mantra of the
bored bartender: "Bud, Bud Light, Miller, Miller
Lite, Coors..."

"No microbrews?" I interrupted. "No good
imports?"

She looked at me, disbelieving. "Honey," she
said. "You didn't come here just for the beer, did
you?"

Well, yes. Like the old saying, I went there just
for the beer. And to a lot of other places. No sym-
pathy is expected, but I wouldn't mind having a
pint for every time somebody heard about this
project and said, "Well, it's a tough job, but somebody's got to do it." Working on this guide *was* a
lot of fun, and provided an intense glimpse of the
rapidly-changing New York bar scene and beer
business, along with the steadily-maturing tastes
of New York beer drinkers.

The idea for this book came from the people at
the Craft Brewers Guild, which represents
dozens of the finest American micros and
gourmet imports sold in and around New York.
So often, someone would have one of these
beers and say, "Hey, this is great. Where can I
buy this?" The Craft Brewers Guild and I hope
this will help answer questions about buying and
drinking good beer in and around New York.

The guide includes listings for 120 bars and
restaurants, and more than 100 deli's, beverage

centers, groceries, supermarkets and good beer stores. The research wasn't all fun, especially when it came to leaving out some places that were pleasant bars or well-run stores but didn't have good beer, or not enough good beer – yet – to merit a listing.

The criteria for listing a bar or restaurant were subjective, largely depending on my own taste, knowledge and experience as a writer who has done many travel and business stories about bars and beer around the world, and as an early investor in and occasional export consultant for the Brooklyn Brewery. I'll be the first to admit to certain prejudices. I like family places where kids are welcome, the food is reasonable and the beer is good. I like places that do oysters on the half shell. I like places that allow cigars, and have the Talking Heads on the sound system. I like places that have old tin ceilings, and where people can talk without being drowned out by tractor pulls on giant TV screens or by loud video games. I like live music, especially jazz and rhythm 'n' blues. More importantly for the reader, every entry in this book – unlike those in many guides – is the result of the author's personal research. I have been to every one of the bars, restaurants and stores reviewed in the book – and many more, like the Pussycat, that didn't make it. I've had beers and hung out in most of the places listed in this book, and made repeated visits to those with the longer reviews and higher ratings. (Indeed, there are those who believe I visited the three-star entries far more times than absolutely necessary for research.)

Speaking of ratings, the reader will note that most of the bar and restaurant entries in this book are adorned with one, two or three stars. Three stars mean it's one of the best places to drink good beer in all of New York, with a extraordinary selection of good beer and a combination of atmosphere and service that is geared toward the serious beer drinker. Two stars mean the place has an outstanding selection of good beer. Many of the two-star entries, it should be pointed out, are also noteworthy for their food. One star means the selection of beer is very good – far superior to that in the usual mainstream bar or restaurant, and well worth making a point to visit.

For bars and restaurants, the ratings criteria included the way a place looks, the atmosphere, the staff's knowledge, service and friendliness, the clientele, food, prices, entertainment and all the other vague factors that make a good bar and/or restaurant. However, one objective factor did dominate: the number and variety of American microbrews and gourmet imports. Places with good selections of draft beer got extra credit. The reviews for a few establishments mention the names of celebrity patrons, but those places got no extra credit in the ratings for bragging about their clientele. Besides, the bars that draw the most celebrities probably are the least likely to drop names. (One thing is certain, however: the actor Matt Dillon is to New York bars in the 1990s what Charles Dickens was to London pubs in the 19th century. Just as so many London publicans today claim, "Dickens used to drink here," there seem to be few Manhattan bars Matt Dillon didn't drink in at some point in the past few years.)

For package stores, the criteria were similarly subjective, but less broad. Cleanliness, brightness and good displays were important, but the selection of beers and service to customers – information about the beers, food advice, newsletters, mix-and-match racks, sampler boxes, special orders, good prices – were more important.

Brewpubs and "landmark" bars have no stars, but are included in the book. The selection of beers at many of the most famous old bars in New York is not particularly distinguished, but those bars were listed anyway because they are such landmarks for beer drinkers. Similarly, few brewpubs have much selection of beer beyond their own brews. Another factor is that most of the brewpubs in and around New York are relatively new, and still have some way to catch up to the generally higher quality of more established brewpubs in the West. All the existing brewpubs were listed, however, because they are of such interest to good beer drinkers. The original New York brewpub, the Manhattan Brewery, was listed in the hope that it will overcome the financial troubles that caused it to close in early 1995. By the time this guide is published, there may be several new brewpubs, including one on Union Square and another just off Times Square. The Brooklyn Brewery is also planning to open an ale brewery with a tasting room on North 11th Street in Williamsburg.

This guide came into being because of the growing number of people interested in good beer. Tastes in beer are changing, obviously. But this guide is also the inevitable victim of those changing tastes and the growing popularity of good beer. The New York good-beer scene is developing so rapidly that some of this guide's entries undoubtedly will be out of date. A few bars and restaurants will have changed hands or closed or decided to become something other than places that sell good beer. Happily, new bars and restaurants will have opened with good beer on their menus, and many more existing establishments, including stores, will have decided to carry more gourmet beer. Some of the one-star and two-star establishments listed in this edition surely will have upgraded themselves to the equivalent of two-star or three-star ratings. The publishers and I are sorry for any inconvenience, and can only promise the disappointed, both those who sell beer and those who drink it, that we welcome updates from them for inclusion in future editions.

In thinking of updates, we encourage readers to exchange information not only with the Craft Brewers Guild – see the information for getting on the mailing list at the back of this book – but with other beer drinkers and with people who sell beer. Many consumers don't realize how closely managers and owners listen to their requests for new, different and better beers. Indeed, virtually all of the package sales outlets listed in the "Stores" section of this book can and will order any beer a customer requests. We also urge readers to talk up good beer among themselves, and not just from barstool to barstool. Share books, newsletters, catalogs and good advertising. Surf the Internet for beer newsgroups, and check out services such as America Online, Prodigy and CompuServe, whose bulletin boards have become valuable sources and means of exchanging information about beer and brewing.

Finally, some acknowledgments. This book, while hardly all-inclusive, would have had considerably less useful information and considerably fewer pointed observations without the ready assistance of so many owners, managers, chefs, wait staff, clerks and other employees of the more than 200 listed bars, restaurants, taverns, saloons, deli's, beer stores, supermarkets and beverage centers.

Apart from depending on the kindness of strangers, my research was also aided by the help of many friends and a few relatives. Mike Paternoster, Mike Sullivan and Keith Jenkins were congenial company at several downtown Manhattan places. Jim Pavia provided valuable insight and Rick Pienciak was a good guide for Staten Island.

People from the Craft Brewers Guild and the Brooklyn Brewery were extremely helpful, both in terms of advice and background information. They include Karyn Broughton, Michele Mitchell, Rich Nowak, Alan Bacchiochi, Gerald Cogdell, Sean Deeks, Bill Manger, Garrett Oliver, Ed Ravn, and especially Steve Hindy, Tom Potter, Jim Munson and Mike Vitale. Steve Hindy, who used to make his living as an editor, and Jim Munson, who probably could if he ever gets out of the beer business, made many valuable suggestions large and small for making this a better and more useful book.

Tony Millionaire's artistic talents were greatly appreciated on the maps. Also, thanks to Milton Glaser – the Chimay Grand Reserve of design, who just keeps getting better – for his work on the cover. And, of course, Ashley Brown and his staff, especially Rosamund Saunders, at Brown Packaging, Liverpool Road, London, England, brought their usual high production and design values to the process of turning a battered, beer-stained manuscript into the sleek book in your hand.

Closer to home, Eleanor Harper provided invaluable assistance by flying in to do grandmother duty during a very busy period of research and writing. My wife, Nancy Bobrowitz, and our children, Lizzie and Jonathan, provided their usual support and good cheer during this project. However, during just a few of those long nights away from home, I would have preferred that they tell callers I was "researching a book" rather than "hitting the bars again."

Tim Harper
Brooklyn, New York
July 1995

HOW TO USE THIS BOOK

This guide is arranged to make it easier to locate
listings by rating, location and type of establishment. The book is divided into two main sec-
tions: bars and restaurants are in the first section, while stores and other packaged beer retail-
ers are in the second.

The entries for bars and restaurants are in
alphabetical order. The indexes on the pages
immediately after this "how to" explanation can
help identify individual bars and restaurants by
various categories. The top-rated bars are listed
under their own index, for example, and so are
fine restaurants, ethnic restaurants, brewpubs,
etc. If you're looking for a good restaurant for
children, find the names under that index and
then look up individual entries for description,
location, phone number and other details.

There are also location indexes, geographic
listings for all the bar and restaurant entries for
Chelsea, for Midtown, for the Upper West Side,
for Brooklyn, etc.

Alternatively, the maps can help identify bars,
restaurants and stores in particular areas. There
are a number of Manhattan maps, along with
others for Brooklyn, Long Island and Westchester and Rockland counties. When planning
an urban plunge into Greenwich Village, for
example, look at the map and plot a route. Or
stick this guide in a pocket (that's why it's this
size) and make up the itinerary *en route*.

The section devoted to stores is not organized
alphabetically. Instead, it lists entries by region:
Manhattan; Brooklyn and Queens; Long Island,
and Westchester/Rockland counties. Some of
the best stores, those with an extraordinary
selection of good beers and outstanding customer service, have entries with written descriptions. The best of the rest, all with very good
selections of beer and superior customer service, merely list the name, address and phone
number of the store.

INDEXES TO BARS AND RESTAURANTS

The Best Beer Bars***

Adobe Blues
Brewsky's
Burp Castle
Cafe Centro Beer Bar
Cafe de Bruxelles
Chumley's
Company B's
d.b.a. 41 first avenue
Dr. Finley's Publick House

East Side Ale House
Kinsale Tavern
Mugs Alehouse
North Star Pub
Peculier Pub
Pugsley's Pub
Ruby's Tap House
Waterfront Ale House

Fine Restaurants With Good Beer

American Festival Cafe
Arizona 206
Brighton Grill
Cafe Centro
Cafe de Bruxelles
Cub Room
First
Gotham Bar and Grill
Gramercy Tavern
Henry's End
Josie's

L'Acajou
Les Halles
London Lennie's
Nosmo King
Oceana
Picholine
Silver Swan
TriBeCa Grill
Tropica
Vong
Zöe

Best for Children

Amsterdam's
Boulevard
Brasserie
City Limits Diner
Company B's
Dr. Finley's Publick House
Firehouse
Grange Hall
Horsefeathers
James Bay Brewing Co.
Jekyll and Hyde
Lefty Louie's
Life Cafe
Lox Around the Clock

McFeeley's
Main Street
Manhattan Chili Co.
Moran's
Park Slope Brewery
Parks' Place
Prince Street Bar
Slaughtered Lamb
Soho Kitchen and Bar
Stubs
Taci International
Teddy's Bar
TGI Friday's
Virgil's Real Barbecue

Best Live Music Places

Adobe Blues	Jules Bistro
Company B's	Knitting Factory
Coopersmith's	Ludlow Street Cafe
Dr. Finley's Publick House	Seven Willow Street
Foffé	Tasca do Porto
Iridium	Teddy's Bar

Best Raw Bars & Seafood

Blue Ribbon	London Lennie's
Brighton Grill	Moran's
Canterbury Ales	Oceana
Fraunces Tavern	Oyster Bar
Hurricane Island	Sidewalkers
James Bay Brewing Co.	Tropica
Johnney's Fish Grill	

Theme Bars

Burp Castle	Jekyll & Hyde Club
Dr. Finley's Publick House	Jekyll & Hyde Pub
Horsefeathers	No-Tell Motel
Jack the Ripper Pub	Slaughtered Lamb Pub

Ethnic Food/Drink

Bar Six	Jules Bistro
Brasserie	Kin Khao
Cafe de Bruxelles	L'Acajou
Cafe Loup	Les Halles
Caffe Buon Gusto	Lox Around the Clock
Caffe di Nonna	Silver Swan
China Grill	Taci International
Foffé	Tasca do Porto
Jimmy Armstrong's Saloon	Vong

New American Cooking

American Festival Cafe	Gotham Bar and Grill
Amsterdam's	Gramercy Tavern
Blue Ribbon	Grange Hall
Cafe Centro	Henry's End
City Limits Diner	McFeeley's
Cub Room	Main Street
Cupping Room Cafe	riverrun
First	TriBeCa Grill
Friend of a Farmer	Zöe

Spicy Food

Adobe Blues
Arizona 206
Firehouse
Ludlow Street Cafe

Manhattan Chili Co.
Nacho Mama's Burritos
Virgil's Real Barbecue

Burgers, Pasta, Pub Grub

Broome Street Bar
Company B's
Chumley's
Croxley Ales
Firehouse
Hi Life Bar and Grill
Hi Life Lounge
Kinsale Tavern
Lazy Boy Saloon
Manchester
Parks' Place

Pete's Tavern
Prince Street Bar
O'Donohue's Tavern
Old Town Bar
Soho Kitchen and Bar
Stubs
Teddy's Bar
Telephone Bar & Grill
TGI Friday's
Tubby's Ivanhoe

Healthy/Organic Dining

Josie's
Nosmo King

Life Cafe

Meat Specialists

Amsterdam's
Frank's Restaurant
Les Halles

Silver Swan
Waterfront Ale House

Brewpubs, Landmark Bars

Fraunces Tavern
James Bay Brewing
Long Island Brewing Co.
McSorley's Old Ale House
Manhattan Brewing Co.
Oyster Bar

Park Slope Brewery
Pete's Tavern
Westside Brewing Co.
White Horse Tavern
Yorkville Brewery
Zip City

LOCATIONS OF BARS AND RESTAURANTS

Downtown, Lower East Side

Fraunces Tavern
Johnney's Fish Grill
Knitting Factory
Ludlow Street Cafe
North Star Pub

Nosmo King
Pugsley's Pub
riverrun
TriBeCa Grill

Soho

Blue Ribbon
Broome Street Bar
Caffe di Nonna
Cub Room
Cupping Room
Kin Khao

Manhattan Brewing Co.
Prince Street Bar
Soho Kitchen and Bar
Tasca do Porto
Zöe

East Village

Brewsky's
Burp Castle
d.b.a 41 first avenue
First
Gotham Bar and Grill

Jules' Bistro
Life Cafe
McSorley's Old Ale House
No-Tell Motel
Telephone Bar and Grill

Greenwich Village

Bar Six
Cafe de Bruxelles
Cafe Loup
Chumley's
Grange Hall

Jack the Ripper Pub
Jekyll and Hyde Pub
Peculier Pub
Slaughtered Lamb Pub
White Horse Tavern

Chelsea

Frank's Restaurant
L'Acajou
Lox Around the Clock

Moran's
Zip City

Gramercy

Gramercy Tavern
Friend of a Farmer
Les Halles

Old Town Bar
Pete's Tavern
Silver Swan

Midtown East

Brasserie	Oceana
Cafe Centro Beer Bar	Oyster Bar
East Side Ale House	Tropica
Manchester	Vong

Midtown West

American Festival Cafe	Jimmy Armstrong's
China Grill	Manhattan Chili Co.
Jekyll and Hyde Club	Virgil's Real Barbecue

Upper East Side

Arizona 206	Kinsale Tavern
Auction House	Lefty Louie's
Brighton Grill	Ruby's Tap House
Hi Life Lounge	Twins
Hurricane Island	Yorkville Brewery

Upper West Side

Abbey Pub	Jake's Dilemma
Amsterdam's	Josie's
Bear Bar	Main Street
Boulevard	Nacho Mama's
Dive Bar	Picholine
Firehouse	Sidewalkers
Hi Life Bar and Grill	Taci International
Iridium	West Side Brewing Co.

Brooklyn/Queens

Brooklyn Inn	Mugs Alehouse
Caffe Buon Gusto	Park Slope Brewing Co.
Foffé	

Stubs

Henry's End	Teddy's Bar
London Lennie's	Waterfront Ale House
McFeeley's	

Long Island

Canterbury Ales
Coopersmith's
Croxley Ales
Dr. Finley's Publick House
James Bay Brewing Co.

Long Island Brewing Co.
Parks' Place
Tubby's
Tubby's Ivanhoe

Staten Island

Adobe Blues

Westchester, Rockland

City Limits Diner
Company B's
Doral Arrowwood
Horsefeathers

Lazy Boy's Saloon
O'Donohue's Tavern
Seven Willow Street
TGI Friday's

MAPS

MAP 1: DOWNTOWN

2 Adobe Blues (63 Lafayette Ave, Staten Island)
9 Blue Ribbon (97 Sullivan)
15 Broome Street Bar (363 W. Broadway)
19 Caffe di Nonna (104 Grand)
29 Cub Room (131 Sullivan)
30 Cupping Room (359 W. Broadway)
40 Fraunces Tavern (54 Pearl)
57 Johnney's Fish Grill (250 Vesey)
60 Kin Khao (171 Spring)
62 Knitting Factory (74 Leonard)
71 Ludlow Street Cafe (165 Ludlow)
76 Manhattan Brewing Co (40-42 Thompson)
81 North Star Pub (93 South Street)
82 Nosmo King (54 Varick)
93 Prince Street Bar and Restaurant (125 Prince)
94 Pugsley's Pub (Washington and Albany)
95 riverrun (176 Franklin)
101 Soho Kitchen and Bar (103 Greene)
104 Tasca do Porto (525 Broome)
108 TriBeCa Grill (375 Greenwich Street)
120 Zöe (90 Prince)

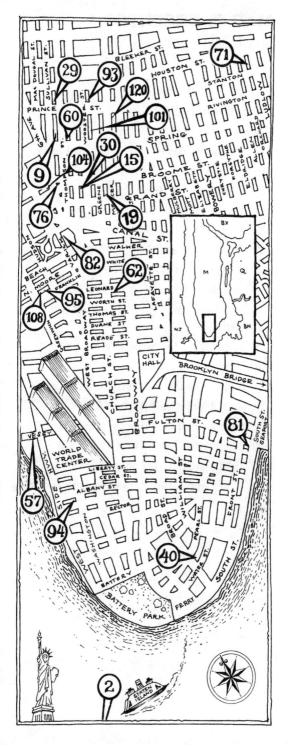

DOWNTOWN

MAP 2: GREENWICH VILLAGE

7 Bar Six (502 Sixth Ave)
12 Brewsky's (43 E. 7th)
16 Burp Castle (41 E. 7th)
18 Cafe de Bruxelles (118 Greenwich Ave)
20 Cafe Loup (105 W. 13th)
24 Chumley's (86 Bedford)
31 d.b.a. 41 first avenue (41 First Ave)
37 First (87 First Ave)
42 Gotham Bar and Grill (12 E. 12th)
44 Grange Hall (50 Commerce)
51 Jack the Ripper Pub (226 W. 4th)
55 Jekyll and Hyde Pub (91 Seventh Ave South)
59 Jules' Bistro (65 St. Mark's Pl)
67 Life Cafe (343 E. 10th)
73 McSorley's Old Ale House (15 E. 7th)
83 No-tell Motel (167 Avenue A)
90 Peculier Pub (145 Bleecker)
100 Slaughtered Lamb Pub (182 W. 4th)
106 Telephone Bar (149 Second Ave)
117 White Horse Tavern (567 Hudson Tavern)

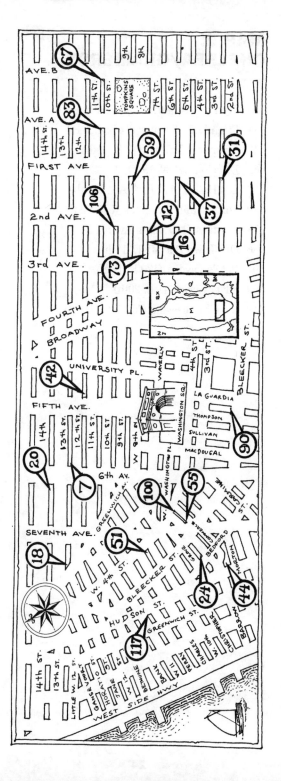

GREENWICH VILLAGE

MAP 3: CHELSEA/GRAMERCY

39 Frank's Restaurant (85 Tenth Ave)
41 Friend of a Farmer (77 Irving Pl)
43 Gramercy Tavern (42 E. 20th)
63 L'Acajou (53 W. 19th)
66 Les Halles (441 Park Ave South)
70 Lox Around the Clock (676 Sixth Ave)
78 Moran's (145 Tenth Ave)
86 Old Town Bar (45 E. 18th)
91 Pete's Tavern (129 E. 18th)
99 Silver Swan (41 E. 20th)
119 Zip City Brewing Co. (3 W. 18th)

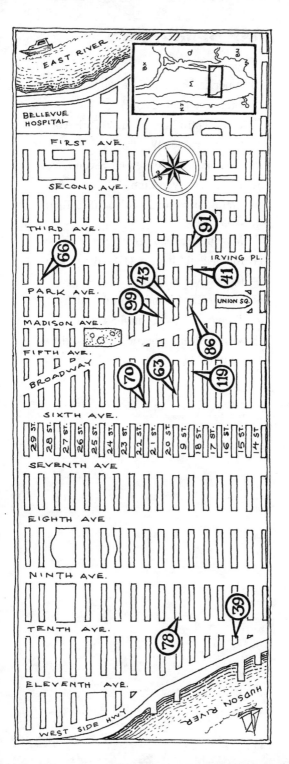

CHELSEA/GRAMERCY

MAP 4: MIDTOWN

3 American Festival Cafe (20 W. 50th)
11 Brasserie (100 E. 53rd)
17 Cafe Centro Beer Bar (200 Park Ave)
23 China Grill (60 W. 53rd)
35 East Side Ale House (961 Second Ave)
54 Jekyll and Hyde Club (1409 Sixth Ave)
56 Jimmy Armstrong's Saloon (875 Tenth Ave)
75 Manchester (920 Second Ave)
77 Manhattan Chili Co. (1500 Broadway)
84 Oceana (55 E. 54th)
87 Oyster Bar (Grand Central Station)
109 Tropica (Grand Central Station)
113 Virgil's Real Barbecue (152 W. 44th)
114 Vong (200 E. 54th)

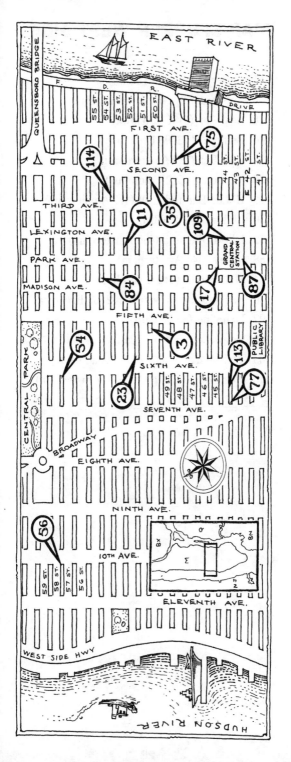

MIDTOWN

MAP 5: UPPER WEST SIDE

1 Abbey Pub (237 W. 105th)
4 Amsterdam's (454 Amsterdam)
8 Bear Bar (2156 Broadway)
10 Boulevard (2398 Broadway)
32 Dive Bar (732 Amsterdam)
36 Firehouse (522 Columbus)
46 Hi Life Bar and Grill (477 Amsterdam)
50 Iridium (44 W. 63rd)
52 Jake's Dilemma (430 Amsterdam)
58 Josie's (344 Amsterdam)
74 Main Street (446 Columbus)
80 Nacho Mama's Burritos (2867 Broadway)
92 Picholine (35 W. 64th)
98 Sidewalkers (12 W. 72nd)
103 Taci International (2841 Broadway)
116 Westside Brewing Co. (340 Amsterdam)

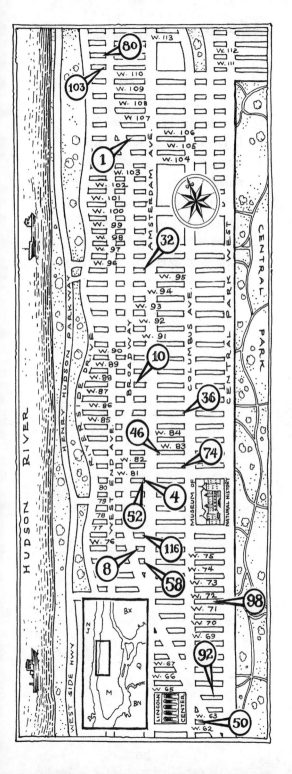

UPPER WEST SIDE

MAP 6: UPPER EAST SIDE

5 Arizona 206 (206 E. 60th)
6 Auction House (300 E. 89th)
13 Brighton Grill (1313 Third Ave)
47 Hi Life Lounge (1340 First Ave)
49 Hurricane Island (1303 First Ave)
61 Kinsale Tavern (1672 Third Ave)
65 Lefty Louie's (1690 York)
96 Ruby's Tap House (1754 Second Ave)
112 Twins (1712 Second Ave)
118 Yorkville Brewery (1359 First Ave)

UPPER EAST SIDE

MAP 7: BROOKLYN

14 Brooklyn Inn (148 Hoyt)
21 Caffe Buon Gusto (151 Montague)
38 Foffé (155 Montague)
45 Henry's End (44 Henry)
72 McFeeley's (847 Union)
79 Mugs Alehouse (125 Bedford)
88 Park Slope Brewery (356 Sixth Ave)
102 Stubs (41 Clark)
105 Teddy's Bar (96 Berry)
115 Waterfront Ale House (136 Atlantic Ave)

BROOKLYN

MAP 8: LONG ISLAND

22 Canterbury Ales (60 Audrey Ave, Oyster Bay)

27 Coopersmith's (615 E. Main, Bayshore)

28 Croxley Ales (129 New Hyde Park Road, Franklin Square)

33 Doctor Finley's Publick House (43 Green, Huntington Village)

53 James Bay Brewing Co. (154 W. Broadway, Port Jefferson)

69 Long Island Brewing Co. (111 Jericho Tpke, Jericho)

89 Parks' Place (121 Mineola Blvd, Mineola)

110 Tubby's (401 Sunrise Hwy, West Islip)

111 Tubby's Ivanhoe (661 Old Willets Path, Hauppauge)

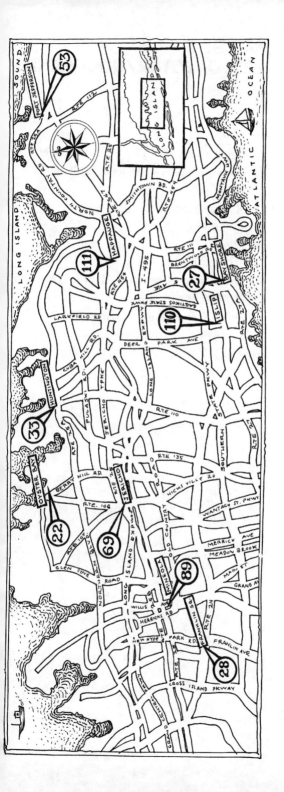

LONG ISLAND

MAP 9:
WESTCHESTER/ROCKLAND

25 City Limits Diner (200 Central Ave, White Plains)

26 Company B's (206 Route 303, Orangeburg)

34 Doral Arrowwood (Anderson Hill Road, Rye Brook)

48 Horsefeathers (94 N. Broadway, Tarrytown)

64 Lazy Boy Saloon (154 Mamaroneck Ave, White Plains)

85 O'Donohue's Tavern (66 Main Street, Nyack)

97 Seven Willow Street (7 Willow, Port Chester)

107 TGI Friday's (240 White Plains Road, Tarrytown)

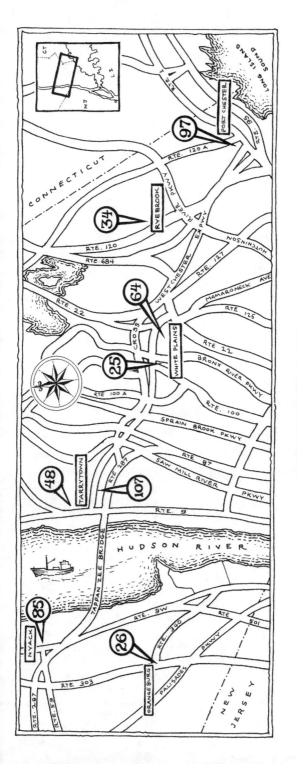

WESTCHESTER/ROCKLAND

BARS and RESTAURANTS

Ratings and Reviews

THE ABBEY PUB*

237 West 105th Street (Broadway)
212-222-8713

Beer for Couples, But Not Hangovers

The Abbey is a dark, quiet little Columbia University neighborhood bar and restaurant that is half a notch below street level and several notches below the glitz of the typical Upper West Side restaurant a mile or two down Broadway.

Paul Holland, the owner, has taken huge strides to supplement the modest menu – several pastas, chicken, burgers, chops, salads, snacks, nearly all for under $10 – with some decidedly immodest beers. He's stocking, and selling, Chimay Rouge, Samuel Smith Nut Brown Ale and Oatmeal Stout, Paulaner Premium Lager (on draft), Brooklyn Lager, Lindemans Framboise and, particularly appropriately, Corsendonk Monk's Brown.

He's laying in the Corsendonk and several other beers in the 25-ounce bottles, and finding a new audience for them by marketing them as "Beer for Couples." He's also reserved one of his coolers solely for seasonal beers. "We have a lot of students and grad students and professors come in, a very educated crowd," Holland says. "They want something different, but they don't know what. We're giving them information and options. Just as our wine list is coordinated to the food, so is the beer list."

"I've found what they say about this really good beer is true," he adds. "I had about six of the Framboise on my birthday, and didn't have any hangover the next day."

Abbaye Notre Dame de Scourmont, otherwise known as Chimay, was the first Belgian monastery to sell its beer commercially.

ADOBE BLUES***

63 Lafayette Avenue, Staten Island
718-720-BLUE

Southwest Food, a Mega Beerlist

This is the best beer joint on Staten Island, no question. Though hard to get to except for those who live on Staten Island – which is good for locals who have little desire to see their hangout overrun by folks from Manhattan or New Jersey – Adobe Blues won't disappoint anyone who takes the trouble to make the trip.

Jim Stayoch and Ken Tirado gutted an old run-down pub and renovated it into a pleasing New York version of a New Mexico roadhouse, complete with a reasonably priced and reasonably spiced menu that is neither Tex nor Mex but something in between. There are only five draft lines, but the list of bottled beer may be the second longest in the entire city, after the Peculier Pub's, with more than 200 bottles, many of them from microbreweries.

Examples: Brooklyn Lager and Brown Ale, Cave Creek Chili Beer, Gator Lager, Dock Street Amber, Harpoon Ale, Old West Amber, Perry's Majestic, Saint Stan's Dark, Pike Place, Simpatico, Stoudt's Abbey Ale and Honey Double Maibock, Tun Tavern, Telluride and Wild Boar Special Amber.

Belgium, England and other countries are well represented, but the proprietors are German fanatics – they're opening a German restaurant, also on Staten Island, with all German drafts – so the wide choice of imports includes: Ayinger Ur-Weisse, Jahrhundert, Altbairish Dunkel and Celebrator; Erdinger Weizenbock, Dortmunder Original and Dark; Rauchenfels; Paulaner Hefe-Weizen; Salvator; Tyrolian Brau, and Wurzburger Dark.

Stayoch says they've been throwing out less than a six-pack a year despite the huge beer list. They move all that beer, Tirado explains, largely through a 1,500-member "99 Bottles of Beer" club that offers prizes such as glasses, hats, shirts and jackets for drinking 33, 66, 99 and 198 bottles. Some guys make a point of going through the entire list once a year. At least.

Adobe Blues becomes a jazz and blues club after midnight on weekends, but perhaps the best night of the week is Wednesday, when the house band cranks up its mix of rhythm and blues at nine o'clock. It's an "open mike," by the way, which means visiting musicians – all accomplished – sit in with the band.

Adobe Blues offers the beer, food and entertainment worthy of any neighborhood bar-restaurant in Manhattan, but without the prices or the attitude.

AMERICAN FESTIVAL CAFE**

20 West 50th Street (5th/6th Aves)
212-246-6699

**5.9 for the Technical Program,
6.0 for Style**

The American Festival Cafe, another jewel in the Restaurant Associates crown of good beer places (see Cafe Centro and Tropica) that also serve great food, is a true destination restaurant in Midtown. Take the elevator down from the middle of Rockefeller Center overlooking the skating rink, and position yourself at a bar or table where you can see all the would-be Kerrigans and Gretzkys, along with a Tonya or two, spinning and sliding across the ice. (In summer the skating rink gives way to tables under umbrellas and becomes part of the restaurant.)

The American Festival Cafe is that rare combination of a good idea that has been well executed: modern and traditional American dishes, prepared with the freshest and highest-quality ingredients, and accompanied by well-chosen lists of American wine and beer.

The beer roster, devoted to micros that are all too often hard to find by themselves in fine restaurants, let alone playing as a team, includes Brooklyn Lager on draft, along with bottles from Catamount, Dock Street, Ebenezer Craft, Geary's, Grant's, Simpatico, Stoudt's and Wild Boar. Plus others, depending on the season.

Like its sister, Cafe Centro's Beer Bar, American Festival features a regular series of Beermakers' Dinners. Recent editions, for the bargain price of $35, featured hosts such as "Buffalo" Bill Owens, Carol Stoudt, Garrett Oliver from Brooklyn, Rob Imeson from Dubuque, Stephen Mason from Catamount, Steve Harrison from Sierra Nevada and Geoffrey Ware from Dock Street.

There may not be another good restaurant anywhere in the country where you can start a meal with Grant's Weis from Washington State, sample starters with Wild Boar Classic Pils from Iowa, wash down the main course with Geary's Ale from Maine or Brooklyn Brown from you-know-where, and wind up with the spectacular Stoudt's Honey Double Maibock from Pennsylvania.

All in a setting amid one of the best-known New York landmarks. For a combination of tourism, midwinter romance or warm-weather *al fresco*, and good food and beer, this is one competition where you can certainly trust the host country's judge.

Duvel is Belgium's best-selling specialty beer, brewed by the third generation of the Moortgat family. The beer is made with a Danish summer barley malt, whole flower Syrian and Saaz hops and is fermented three times. A sign on the brewery in massive red letters reads, "Ssshhh...Duvel is ripening here."

AMSTERDAM'S*

454 Amsterdam Avenue (80th/81st)
212-925-6166

Leader of the Rotisserie League

On the Yupper West Side, where restaurants tend to come and go, Amsterdam's has been a fixture since the early 1980s, and is showing no signs of fading. The menu is large and creative, and the food – whether vegetarian or mainline meat or somewhere in between – is very rarely disappointing.

The beers include Brooklyn Brown, Stoudt's Gold, Harpoon IPA and Young's Oatmeal Stout on draft, along with a good selective list of bottled micros. There are always some fine seasonals on draft or in bottles listed on the blackboard at the entrance.

Besides its terrific french fries and the open kitchen opposite the bar, where you can watch your meat grill or roast over open flames, Amsterdam's is perhaps best known for being kid-friendly. It's not unusual to go in and find virtually every table except for the deuces filled with families. From teens to babes in arms, children are welcome. The wait staff are used to dealing with kids, and do the right things before the parents ask. There are even baby seats.

Bill Owens is one of those rare guys who has become well known in two different fields. As a photographer, he did the classic book *Suburbia*. As a brewer, his Buffalo Bill's Pumpkin Ale is an autumn favorite, and his Alimony Ale is "the bitterest beer in America." He's got a good start on a third career, publishing *American Brewer* and *Beer, The Magazine*.

ARIZONA 206✶✶

206 E. 60th Street (2nd/3rd Aves)
212-838-0440

Southwest Via the East Side

Arizona is the flagship of this four-restaurant complex, a place with a rough-hewn look but sophisticated touches, particularly on the food and beer menus. James Oliver, the manager, has worked hard to bring good beer to the conservative East Side, and it's paid off.

Realizing that micros and good imports (1) appeal to his upscale clientele, (2) complement the spicy food and (3) give him a better markup, Oliver has seen beer rise from 4 percent to 9 percent of his revenue and the *New York Times* give Arizona a three-star review that cites the match between the beer list and chef David Walzog's often spectacular menu.

Among the 30 bottles – "No Bud, no Bud Light, not even Rolling Rock," Oliver says – the only "mainstream" beer is Amstel Light. His better sellers include Pig's Eye, Sierra Nevada, Wild Goose and Wild Boar, but Oliver also offers imports such as Chimay and micro seasonals such as Brooklyn Black Chocolate Stout – on draft, if and when he can get them.

Unlike the staff in many busy restaurants – and this bar, with seating and standing for up to 40, is jammed most nights – Arizona's servers are coached on the beer list. Oliver has regular tastings for the staff, and many of them have gone from being snobs about beer to being beer snobs. "The more we tasted, the more our palettes developed," Oliver says. And the more beer he ordered. Oliver himself, originally a wine man, is so into beer he now goes to the annual Great American Beer Festival in Denver in search of new brews.

If you're early enough or patient enough, Arizona's fireplace at the front of the bar is one of the best wintertime places on the Upper East Side to warm up inside and out.

AUCTION HOUSE*

300 E. 89th Street (1st/2nd Aves)
212-427-4458

Ranging the Upper East Side

This is a bar that probably could exist – and do very well, thank you – only in Manhattan's Silk Stocking District. It's a small place that looks like some rich old widow's parlor, with its tapestry designs, expensive-looking upholstered furniture and people who have obviously spent time on their look. It's a good late-night place, especially for hockey fans (but don't show up waving a rubber chicken or wearing a Mark Messier mask) since it's a New York Rangers hangout. The three draft lines often include Saranac Black and Tan and Sierra Nevada Pale Ale, and the bottles include Chimay. The place will probably soon stock more good brews as its customers become more beer-sophisticated.

BAR SIX**

502 Sixth Avenue (12th/13th)
212-691-1363

French Flavor, American Taste

A gem of a French-Mediterranean bistro, Bar Six opened in 1994 and quickly became a neighborhood fixture. With a distinctive feel reminiscent of a backstreets Paris *zinc* or *tabac*, Bar Six has a good working-class French menu with what manager Gary Lewis – no, nobody calls him Jerry Lewis, even the French customers – terms a "specialty" in American micros and gourmet imports. That's largely due to Diana Van Buren, the managing partner; she's a wine expert who is expanding her expertise to good beer.

There are only two draft lines, but they're Sierra Nevada Stout and Brooklyn Lager, and barely a dozen bottled beers, but they include Rogue, Harpoon, Saranac, Sierra Nevada and several Chimays. A couple of seasonals are usually on hand, such as Sierra Nevada Celebration and Affligem Noel.

There's cool jazz on the system, and a rack full of magazines for customers who, in the French style, want to sip and read at the 12 stools along the front bar. There's never going to be any pressure to order food or take a table, though that's not a bad idea. At night Bar Six becomes quite a party scene, with an emphasis on the latest street fashions. Besides being a spot to check out next year's fashion trends, this place offers an authentic French feel *sans* pretension but *avec* some great beer.

BEAR BAR**

2156 Broadway (75th/76th)
212-362-2145

Micros and Music

The Bear Bar bills itself as "The Micro Brewery Capital of the West Side," and nobody seems to be arguing, though some (see Jake's Dilemma) might. The Bear, an L-shaped no-frills beer bar, offers more than 70 beers, including Anchor Steam, Dock Street, Catamount, Celis, Geary's, Grant's, Harpoon, New England and Telluride. The draft beers include Pete's, Sierra Nevada Pale Ale and Saranac Black and Tan.

The Bear Bar, with its three TV sets (including one bigscreen), stone and blonde-wood chalet styling, big bear statues and loud music, appeals to a youngish crowd, or at least the kind of crowd that still goes to rock concerts on a regular basis. A lot of the talk centers on performers either in town or coming to town. An appearance by Willie Nelson or other name acts at the Beacon, down Broadway in the next block, can have the place pulsating before and after the show. The draft beer is served in plastic cups, like at a concert.

Another Bear Bar is opening on the Upper East Side.

BLUE RIBBON*

97 Sullivan Street (Spring/Prince)
212-274-0404

Small and Friendly

Blue Ribbon is an unpretentious, relaxed Soho place with a good local reputation for chef/owner Eric Bromberg's eclectic menu including steaks, fish, potato pancakes, gumbo, tofu and highly-touted pirogies – "comfort food," according to *Zagat*. With its above-average fare and average prices, this is also a popular Sunday brunch spot. There is a raw bar for oysters and clams on the half shell.

The draft beers include Saranac Gold and Sierra Nevada Pale Ale, while the bottles include Chimay, Ayinger and Paulaner. With its good food, fair prices and late hours (open til 4 a.m. even during the week), this is a place where food professionals, including well-known chefs, tend to gather to eat after closing their own kitchens. Closed Mondays, by the way.

BOULEVARD*

2398 Broadway (88th)
212-874-7400

Solid All-Purpose Broadway Bistro

Locals use Boulevard quite successfully for both a bar and a restaurant. And why not? The food is a good mix of Tex-Mex, pasta, seafood and burgers for reasonable prices, children are welcome and the oval bar is a fine place to meet folks or sit and read. The 20 or so beers include Grant's Apple Honey Ale, Grant's Spiced Ale, Catamount Amber, Saranac Black and Tan, Pete's Wicked Ale, Harpoon and Dock Street.

More could and should be done with the draft lines, however. There are six of them, but Saranac Golden Pilsner and Samuel Adams are the only beers on draft worth mentioning. And no self-respecting bar should join in the conspiracy by printing a beer list that counts Red Dog as a Wisconsin microbrew. Everyone knows that the so-called "Plank Road Brewery" is just Miller hoping to disguise itself in the same way that Anheuser-Busch tries to hide a Bud in (red) wolf's clothing.

BRASSERIE*

100 East 53rd Street (Park/Lex)
212-751-4840

A Slice of the Fifties in the Fifties

You half expect to see Ava Gardner or Gene Tierney or Gwen Verdon gliding down the entry stairs in their little hats and serious coats, on the arm of David Niven or Cary Grant or Clark Gable. This French brasserie still evokes the style of the 1950s, when it opened, and it conjures up a New York of postwar optimism and boom, of movies such as *Funny Face, On the Town* and *Damn Yankees*.

From burgers to cassoulet to entrecote, main courses are in the $10-20 range. The two dozen beers include a number of solid European choices, such as Pinkus Ur Weizen, and a few regional American brews. Ask about unlisted specials and seasonals, such as Samichlaus, the Swiss brew that is widely regarded as the strongest beer – up to 16 percent alcohol by volume – in the world. Brasserie, by the way, is open 24 hours a day, seven days a week, and is a definite candidate for breakfast either to start the day or at the end of a night out.

> **The British have a saying, "Life is not all beer and skittles."**

BREWSKY'S***

43 East 7th Street (2nd/3rd Aves)
212-420-0671

Just Here for the Beer

This bar is a must stop for beer geeks, snobs, aficionados, experts – whatever you want to call folks who want beer of the highest quality and surroundings of the lowest quality. Well, not lowest quality, maybe…let's just say a certain unadorned quality.

Small, with tape holding the stuffing in the plastic seats of its bar stools, Brewsky's is the down-and-dirty antithesis of Burp Castle's "heaven" for beer drinkers next door. It's as if Jerry Kuziw, who owns both Brewsky's and Burp Castle, couldn't decide whether to go upscale and refined, or downscale and no-frills. So he did both, which makes sense to all of us who sometimes feel like behaving while we drink, and at other times don't want to worry about spilling a little onto the sawdust on the floor.

But nobody spills too much at Brewsky's. Not when the eight draft lines deliver beer such as Harpoon Stout, Paulaner Hefe-Weizen, Salvator and Alpine Extreme, and seasonals such as Harpoon Winter Warmer. The 150 bottled beers include varieties carrying the brand names Ayinger, Breckenridge, Boon (Framboise, Gueuze and Faro Pertotale), Catamount, Celis, Chimay, Corsendonk, Duvel, Fischer, Grant's, Liefmans, Lindemans, Old Growler, Old Heurich, Pete's, Pike Place, Rodenbach, Samuel Smith's and Scaldis. And more.

Brewsky's is the sort of place where guys in suits talk beer with guys in flannel shirts, and both occasionally slide their pints slightly off to the side and plop their arms on the bar for a good old-fashioned round of arm wrestling. The door creaks loudly every time it's opened; there are photos of celebrities old and new on the wall, some of whom actually may have been to Brewsky's, along with a world-class collection of beer mats, cans and other beerphernalia. The most definitive decorating flourish is the mangy stuffed deer head wearing a dusty old red, white and blue campaign hat. Brewsky's sells a lot of hats, T-shirts, stickers and decals to beer heads, nuts, geeks, aficionados, etc., so that other beer geeks, nuts, etc., can tell they've been there.

Kuziw hires only fellow beer nuts, heads, geeks, aficionados, experts, etc., to work behind the bar, and these guys are always happy to swap stories about when, where, with whom, how and why – well, why is never really an issue – they have tasted different beers. You want to talk home brewing? The next stool probably has a home brewer on it, and so does the stool after that. Just don't interrupt the arm wrestling.

BRIGHTON GRILL*

1313 Third Avenue (75th/76th)
212-988-6663

Upper East Side Seafood

Favored by many 30s-and-older professionals, Brighton Grill is known for its genteel atmosphere, good service, fine food and – for this part of town, anyway – reasonable prices. Tom Ganley, the chef, makes a different paella every day, and the trout and salmon are smoked in-house. Unlike all too many Manhattan restaurants these days, Brighton Grill makes its own desserts, and even bakes its own bread on the premises.

Brighton Grill concentrates more on wine than beer, but more good beer is slowly making its way onto the menu because of customers' demands, including Harpoon, Brooklyn and Sierra Nevada. This has been rated one of the top 100 restaurants in Manhattan, and reservations are strongly suggested for parties of three or more on week nights. Incidentally, that's a mural on the wall, copied by a New York artist from an ancient Phoenician design.

BROOKLYN INN*

148 Hoyt Street (Bergen), Brooklyn
718-625-9741

Pre-Dating the Bridge

Established in 1851, this is one of the places where the workers who built the Brooklyn Bridge could relax after work. It's still a simple tavern with a solid feel, from the great 20-foot tin ceilings to the elaborate carving on what may be the finest old mahogany bar in New York. The wood floor creaks en route to the pool table in the back room or to the eight taps that offer Brooklyn Lager and Brown Ale, Pilsner Urquell, Harp and Bass.

BROOME STREET BAR*

363 West Broadway (Broome)
212-925-2086

Soho's Gateway to the Holland Tunnel

Looking at Soho today, it's hard to believe that barely 20 years ago the area was more run-down industrial than trendy-artsy. Among the lofts and factories that became shops, galleries and expensive apartments, Kenn's Broome Street Bar was a pioneer when it opened back in 1972.

Today the bar is a favorite for neighborhood folks and people who park near the tunnel for good getaways. With a solid menu built around half-pound burgers, Kenn's offers about three dozen beers, eight of them on draft, including a number of micros and imports such as Black Dog Ale, Pete's, London Pride and Pilsner Urquell. This is also one of the easiest bars in Soho for getting in conversation with the regulars, many of whom are as chatty as they are devoted to the joint.

BURP CASTLE***

41 East 7th Street (2nd/3rd Aves)
212-982-4576

The Temple of Beer

That's what owner Jerry Kuziw calls Burp Castle: his Temple of Beer. The flip side of Brewsky's, his other bar next door, Burp Castle is just as much a must on any serious beer drinker's tour of Manhattan.

Like Brewsky's, Burp Castle is small. There the similarity ends, save for all the good beer. The waiters and bartenders are all dressed in monks' habits, and so is the doorman who apparently enforces the sign at the entrance that reads: "No One Under 25 Admitted." While it surely must be rare for the door-monk to actually card anyone, there's probably not much need, either. Beyond a few banker types in their late twenties, most of the patrons are obviously in their thirties, forties and beyond, and there's not a flannel shirt or backwards baseball cap in sight. While Brewsky's crowd is mostly male, Burp Castle has more women and couples.

The stools, tables and chairs are all polished to a dark sheen. There is no sawdust on the floor, nor a single deer head in sight. Instead, the walls are painted with murals – the heavenly host and entourage, shipwrecks, feasts, market days – that give the place a medieval flavor. The piped-in music, often Gregorian chants or Vivaldi or madrigals or something else pre-Jolson, completes the grotto effect.

There's a sign that says no cigar smoking, but it's not unusual to see somebody lighting up a stogie right in front of it. "As long as it's small," a monk shrugs.

The monks glide between tables and bar, where they growl, "Gimme a pail," and you half expect the bartender to hand over a foamy bucket of beer until you realize the order is for a Corsendonk Pale, in the large bottle. The beer menu, printed in a computerized version of Olde

English script with the information that Burp Castle is "Operated by the Brewist Monks," lists a wide selection of other Belgian Trappist and Abbey beers, including six different Chimay entries, five Corsendonks and several Boon Lambics. The Liefmans lineup includes three brown ales, and Lindemans four.

Besides the many other Belgian beers (Orval, Rodenbach, Witkap, Duvel, etc.) and some good choices from Germany (Ayinger), from France (St. Amand, Castelain) and England (Samuel Smith's, Thomas Hardy's), Burp Castle's American micros include Sierra Nevada (four brews), Celis (three), Catamount, Stoudt's, Telluride and others.

The draft beers change regularly, and are often all special or seasonal brews. For example, a typical cold-weather evening (Burp Castle usually doesn't open until late afternoon) might offer choices such as Sierra Nevada Celebration Ale, Rogue Mogul, Paulaner Hefe-Weizen, Paulaner Salvator, Pete's Winter Brew, Samuel Adams Winter Lager and Young's Winter Ale.

When, not if, you're in the mood for murals, lutes and lyres, quiet talk and a worshipful attitude toward some of the world's best beers, the temple awaits.

In medieval England, the nobility were the only ones who could afford to drink, and they often ended up under the table. Hence the saying, "Drunk as a lord."

CAFE CENTRO
BEER BAR***

MetLife Building, 200 Park Avenue (45th)
212-818-1333

Beer Off the Rails

Restaurant Associates, the company that owns Cafe Centro, is to be applauded for creating the Beer Bar. It is part of the larger restaurant but has its own beer list, its own limited, cheaper but still good menu and even its own entrance (at 45th and Vanderbilt). Cafe Centro is a highly regarded restaurant that is busy well into the evening, while the Beer Bar, utilitarian in its transportation-theme design with Art-Deco flourishes, is more commuter-oriented.

Lunch at the Beer Bar is a real value (burgers, pasta, chicken, veal, etc., $10-15) by Cafe Centro's high standards, but in the afternoon and evening only appetizers are available. But who's eating anyway? The Beer Bar jumps after work and in the early evenings; the old yuppie scene of the 1980s may be dead, but this is not where they went to die. Singles, couples and groups of men and women from the nearby advertising, publishing, law and financial firms gather at the Beer Bar to make friends before catching their trains or starting lives together, whichever happens first. Things slow down at the Beer Bar after 8 p.m., and the place closes at 11 o'clock.

Bottled beers include Catamount Porter, Ebenezer Craft Pale Ale, Grant's Celtic, Lindemans Framboise, Paulaner Hefe-Weizen, and seasonal specials such as Stoudt's Honey Double Maibock and Samuel Smith's Winter Welcome.

The 10 draft lines (the managers wanted to put in 25, but couldn't because of all those trains in the basement) are well rotated, and often include

Brooklyn, Saranac, Sierra Nevada and prized imports such as Young's Ramrod.

What really sets the Beer Bar apart is the management's determination not only to match its beer with its food and vice versa, but also to provide service and education for the good beer drinker.

A prime example is the series of Beermakers' Dinners held throughout the fall, winter and spring. This was the menu for a recent one: Hors d'oeuvres including sole goujonnettes, chicken strudel and potato skins were served with Celis White, Lindemans Kriek and Rauchenfels Steinbier. Then came vegetable and pasta soup with Frank Boon Gueuze and Young's Ramrod, and roasted chicken and mashed potatoes with Brooklyn Brown. The chocolate in pistachio sauce was served with Samuel Smith's Imperial Stout (an extraordinary match, by the way) followed by Thomas Hardy's Ale as a digestif.

The price was $32, a remarkable value, particularly considering that the host was Michael Jackson, who gave an amusing little talk before dinner and then discussed each beer as it was served, digressing as only he can. Restaurant Associates Vice President John Harding has scheduled many other acknowledged beer experts and well-known brewers to host these dinners, including Belgian specialist Don Feinberg, Bert Grant, James Young, Jackie Bateman and Lambic maven John Hansell of *The Malt Advocate*.

The Beer Bar also offers free tastings of new drafts, and is considering barrel tastings – setting up several barrels and letting customers pull their own pints, as many as they want, for a set price. When you go to the Beer Bar – and if you're reading this, you should go – join the Beer Club, which puts you on the mailing list for Beermakers' Dinners, and other beer-related events around New York, and entitles you to a free beer on your birthday (and perhaps a free round for your friends).

CAFE DE BRUXELLES***

118 Greenwich Avenue (W. 13th)
212-206-1830

Not Quite Bruges, But Close Enough

Part French *zinc* bar and part Belgian country inn, this is a truly great restaurant in the West Village. The owners, chef Thierry Moity and hostess Patricia Moity, seem as amazed as anybody that they've managed to run a restaurant together – this one for more than a decade – and stay happily married. It's certainly easy to tell that they like their work. The grilled meat, stews, pate, sausage and, of course, mussels and fries make this the most authentic, and best, Belgian-Northern French restaurant in the city.

As befitting any great Belgian restaurant, there is also a great beer menu. The two dozen-plus beers include Corsendonk, Witkap, Rodenbach Grand Cru, Chimay, Duvel, Orval, Kwak, Blanche de Bruges, Affligem, St. Sebastian and Saison Dupont.

Thierry prepares fully one-third of his dishes, particularly the hearty "country" fare, with ingredients from his beer menu. He also trains his staff to offer tips on what beer goes best with what dishes. To him, the most puzzling thing about the restaurant business in New York is that his competitors haven't caught on to the beer-food connection. "We've been waiting 10 years for everyone to catch up," he says. If he and Patricia keep doing what they're doing, it's unlikely that any other Belgian restaurant in New York will ever catch up.

The brick and lace-curtain dining room seats 70, while the bar has stools for 15. Lunch is noon to 3 p.m. Tuesday through Saturday, dinner 5-11:30 p.m. during the week and until midnight on Friday and Saturday. There's also a Sunday brunch. If you're going for brunch, or on a weekend evening, it's advisable to phone ahead.

In all, this is one of the best-run restaurants, and one of the best dining values, anywhere in

New York. Particular recommendations include the lamb, the beef stew in beer and the seafood stew. The fries, served Belgian-style in a metal tumbler with plenty of mayonnaise for dipping, are terrific. And make sure to leave room for dessert – beer, food or both. For people who love food and love beer and are into the matching of beer and food, Cafe de Bruxelles is an essential part of their education.

CAFE LOUP*

105 W. 13th Street (Sixth Ave)
212-255-4746

French in the Village

Depending on your route, this could be the first of many French restaurants you encounter heading into Greenwich Village. It's a busy little place in a busy part of town, where the bustle of Union Square and 14th Street start to blend into the characterful and charming – but no less busy – byways of the Village.

The menu is reasonably priced and deserves its strong reputation, and the management has a long history of featuring imported beers. The current beer list offers a selection of Belgian and English beers in bottles, including Duvel, Orval Trappist and Sam Smith's Nut Brown, Taddy Porter and seasonals. But it would be *tres bien* to have a stronger choice of beers on the four draft lines. "Loup," by the way, means wolf in French.

Residents of California's Anderson Valley speak a dialect called Boontling, which is used on the Anderson Valley Brewing Co. labels. Of Barney Flats Oatmeal Stout, for example, a local might say, "It's not just shy sluggin' gorms neemer!"

CAFFE BUON GUSTO*

151 Montague Street (Clinton/Henry), Brooklyn
718-624-3838

The Heights of Trendiness

With its cool front bar and white-and-green din-ing room, this Italian restaurant has become one of the twin pillars, along with neighboring Foffé, of the Brooklyn Heights cafe society among the 25-to-35 set. It's a great place to gather any time in the afternoon or evening, either as a destina-tion for dinner or as a staging area for an urban plunge. It's one of those places where everyone seems to be good looking. There's Sierra Nevada Pale Ale and Brooklyn Lager on draft.

CAFFE DI NONNA*

104 Grand Street (Mercer)
212-925-5488

Pasta in Soho

Caffe di Nonna is a former bakery – the old tile walls are still there – that became an Italian restaurant in September 1994. Unlike many of the trendy new eateries in Soho, this is a relaxed, low-key place, from the small bar up front to the semi-open kitchen in back.

The sound system plays the kind of jazz that goes with good food and good conversation. The menu features chicken and seafood besides some innovative pasta dishes, and the beer menu lists Moretti, Harpoon Light, Duvel, Tucher Hefe-Weizen, Samuel Smith's Nut Brown Ale, Affligem Dobbel and Brooklyn Lager.

> Germany has about one-third of the world's breweries, and half of them are in Bavaria.

CANTERBURY ALES**

60 Audrey Avenue, Oyster Bay
516-922-3614

Well Worth the Pilgrimage

Oyster Bay is famous for its annual fall festival of oysters and beer, not necessarily in that order. Fortunately, Canterbury Ales ably meets those basic requirements of civilization even when the festival isn't on. From the fresh sea air in the parking lot to the long bar to the Sagamore Library, filled with photos of Teddy Roosevelt when he lived on nearby Sagamore Hill, this is a classic seafood restaurant.

A blackboard explains the half-dozen different types of oysters on offer, and the beer menu runs to more than 100 entries, including double-digits from Belgium, England and Germany. Some examples: St. Sixtus Abbey Ale, Lindemans Peche, Affligem Dobbel, Orval Trappist, Duvel, Corsendonk Brown, Royal Oak, several Sam Smith's, Celebrator Doppelbock, Paulaner Hefe-Weizen, Pinkus Ur Pils, Hacker Pschorr and Spaten. Drinkers into vintage beer should ask about the bottles of Thomas Hardy's Ale that have been laid down; they include some ordinarily hard-to-find years.

The American micros in bottles include Grant's Celtic and Scottish Ales, Old Peconic Hampton Ale, Catamount Porter, Dixie Blackened Voodoo and Cave Creek Chili Beer. The draft beer includes Saranac, Catamount, Pilsner Urquell, Old Foghorn and Whitbread.

Porter beer, lighter in body than stouts, was so named because it was the beverage of choice among English porters who worked the streets and docks, carrying heavy bundles and bales and then refreshing themselves with a beer.

CHINA GRILL*

60 West 53rd Street (CBS Building)
212-333-7788

If You'd Rather Have Chinese

Despite being located on the ground floor of the CBS headquarters on Sixth Avenue, known to the serfs who toil there in network anonymity as Black Rock, this upscale Chinese place has never caught on as a hangout for Dan Rather and the other talent. It is popular for many others on expense-account lunches, however.

The long bar is easily reached from entrances on either 53rd or 52nd, and is a popular after-work gathering place for the Midtown media mob, including the news agencies and many magazines based in the area. There's a reasonable selection of imports and micros, but you might have to press a bartender to recall just what they are.

CHUMLEY'S***

86 Bedford Street (Barrow)
212-675-4449

Speak Easy and Carry a Big Pint

The site of a speakeasy back in the 1920s, the Chumley's of the 1990s draws people for its draft microbrews the way the zoot-suiters and flappers of Prohibition used to pack in for bathtub gin.

The 22 draft lines, which take up virtually the whole wall behind the small bar, offer an all-star lineup of Eastern micros, along with occasional visitors from the Midwest and mountain states. The Brooklyns, the Harpoons and the Saranacs are the heavy – and in a couple of cases light, as in calories – hitters in the lineup, but there are always some home runs from near and far.

Chumley's has no pretense of being anything other than a beer bar – sawdust, tables with names carved over names, toilets that work OK most of the time – that also serves some good food at reasonable prices. The pub grub is a step up from the usual wings 'n' rings, with roast duck, ribeye steak and a good selection of grilled seafood, all in the $15 range. The lobster special is a famous bargain.

The dining room, the biggest room in the place, was at one time, in its pre-speakeasy days, a blacksmith's shop. Certainly some solid beer relationships – as Norm on Cheers used to say, "Boy meets beer, boy drinks beer, boy meets another beer..." – are forged there. Remarkably but thoughtfully, there's also a very good selection of herbal teas for companions who are somewhat more genteel than the customer trying to work across America via those 22 draft lines, one by one. The cold box, by the way, is a 15-foot-by-15-foot earth-walled pit under the bar.

Chumley's can be crowded in the evenings, particularly on or near the weekend. But at quieter times, in the afternoons, it's not unusual to see dogs or kids scampering around in the sawdust while the people responsible for them perch on the seven bar stools. For a respite from the crowds, there's also a little room off to the right with a few tables.

One of the most challenging things about Chumley's is finding it. There's no sign, so more than one would-be customer has looked around at the otherwise unmarked door that should be 86 Bedford Street, and then walked away puzzled. Give the door a push, however, and you're in the dining room.

For those bringing friends to Chumley's for the first time, a favorite trick is to act like you don't know where the place is, and stumble around the corner, mumbling and squinting and saying, "It has to be around here somewhere," onto Barrow Street. Go into the little courtyard of the apartment building there, past the residents' garbage cans and mailboxes. While your friends are trying to get you to retreat because this has to be the wrong place, push on the unmarked black wooden door and find yourself face to face with the bar and 22 glorious taps. However it's done, getting to Chumley's is a must for good beer drinkers.

CITY LIMITS DINER**

200 Central Avenue (Route 119),
White Plains
914-686-9000

A Diner And So Much More

From a passing car, City Limits looks like a typical New York-New Jersey roadside diner. It's not. Opened in May 1994 by the same folks who operate Oceana in the city, it was designed to look like a diner. And the menu, at first glance, looks like a typical all-but-the-kitchen-sink diner menu.

But look more closely. The dishes are created and prepared by chefs from the Culinary Institute of America, with a flair and creativity uncommon among many white-tablecloth restaurants, let alone diners. At City Limits, the term "diner" is meant to tell customers that meals are served around the clock. There's also a good and extensive children's menu.

City Limits, which does occasional beer dinners, takes its beer seriously. There are several drafts at the small bar just to the right of the campy giant coffee cup and donut at the entrance, but the selection of 57 bottled beers is the real draw. They include Duvel, Geary's, Harpoon, Lindemans, MacAndrews, New England, Pike Place, Saranac, Scaldis, Samuel Smith's and Stoudt's.

Along with the giant coffee cup, the decor is something like The Jetsons meets Alice, with the big red neon signs for "Cokes" and "Pies," and the silvery hourglass light fixtures. For a true savoring of the suburbs, the outdoor patio in summertime provides nice views of the traffic heading to and from the Tappan Zee Bridge.

COMPANY B'S***

206 Route 303 (S. of Route 340),
Orangeburg
914-365-6060

SubBEERban Bliss

"I know it's in the suburbs," the committed city dweller was telling his buddies. "But I tell you, I drive into that big parking lot, walk in there and see all those tap handles and I get shivers down my spine."

Company B's is a true beer mecca. With 52 draft lines at last count (six or seven more were planned by the end of 1995) and a different beer on each line, this big, airy place draws beer pilgrims from all over New York and New Jersey. A partial list: Rogue-N-Berry, Blizzard Bock, New England Oatmeal Stout, Hudson Lager, Dock Street Amber, Wild Goose Amber, Harpoon Light, Big Indian Porter, Woodstock Mai-Bock, New England Atlantic Amber, New Haven Blackwell Stout, Stoudt's Fest, Fuller's ESB, Anchor Porter and Ichabod Crane Pumpkin.

The American micros in bottles include: Catamount American Wheat; Geary's Ale; Grant's Celtic Ale, Imperial Stout, India Pale Ale and Scottish Ale; Harpoon Ale and Golden Lager; Mr. Mike's Light Ale; Olde Heurich; Pike Place; Telluride, and Saranac Pale Ale.

Bottled imports: Brasseurs; Castelain Blonde; Celebrator Doppelbock; Chimay Grand Reserve and Rouge; Corsendonk Pale Ale and Monk's Brown Ale; Duvel; Liefmans Frambozen and Goudenband; Lindemans Kriek, Framboise and Peche; Orval Trappist; Pinkus Ur Pils and Ur Weizen; Spaten Weiss; Samichlaus; Rodenbach, and Samuel Smith's Nut Brown Ale, Pale Ale and Winter Welcome.

The long bar, shaped like a question mark, leads to a party room, video games and a couple of pool tables at one end, and to the large dining room, with well-spaced light-wood tables and booths, at the other end. The food is a pleasant mix of pub grub, burgers, pizza, salads and grilled ribs and steaks, all good and all reasonably priced. The crowd is a mix of white collar and families during the day and early evening, and late 20s on up in the evenings.

There's a gift shop and a mailing list and a Beer Challenge; when the bartenders log your 100th beer on the files they keep behind the bar, your name is immortalized on a plaque above the fireplace. You also get your choice of a Company B's jacket from the gift shop or a half-yard glass of your own to take home. For $50, you can join the Mug Club, which entitles you to a discount on each pint.

There's acoustic music on weeknights and a band on weekends, except on nights when there are beer dinners. Hosts have included Michael Jackson, Bert Grant and Steve Hindy.

COOPERSMITH'S**

615 E. Main Street, Bayshore
516-666-0011

"Long Island's Best Live Acoustic Music"

That's Coopersmith's motto, but be forewarned that the music is only on Friday and Saturday nights. The good beer, however, is every night at this long, narrow bar in a small strip shopping center. The place is open from 11 a.m. to 4 a.m., and there's a menu that includes burgers starting at $2 and meals such as meatloaf with mashed potatoes and a vegetable for $5. But the 17 draft lines are what draw the good beer drinkers. "Nothing's on for more than 10 days," says owner Dennis Bennett.

It's a discerning crowd, a little older (23 or older is Bennett's requirement) than at many of the louder nearby places. People stop in before or after a movie, for a quick and inexpensive bite or a couple of pints of Dock Street Pilsner, Elm City Ale, Dinkel Acker Dark, Evil Eye Ale, Sam

Adams Double Bock, Paulaner Hefe-Weizen or one of the other good beers on draft.

This is an unpretentious place that has become a focal point for good beer on this part of the South Shore.

CROXLEY ALES**

129 New Hyde Park Road, Franklin Square
516-326-9542

"Long Island's Original Ale House"

Co-owner Chris Werle wasn't satisfied with this good bar with English pub accents, including a red London phone box, and an admirable row of 29 draft lines. "We're expanding," he says. "We're going up to 75 to 100 draft lines."

He opened the bar with 18 draft lines and thought that was "an over-abundance." But now, he realizes, "It's impossible to have an over-abundance of draft lines." Those original lines were packed with English ales and stouts, but as more good American micros became available they began pushing off the English beers. "We didn't want to choose between English and American beers, so if we had more draft lines we wouldn't have to choose," Werle reasons.

Croxley's is a comfortable place, with a few tables and some roomy booths. The typical bar food is enhanced by some good English additions, including bangers and mash, chicken pot pie, shepherds' pie and fish and chips made with fresh fish that are cut and battered in tempura only after the order is placed. "Nothing is pre-made," Werle promises.

A few of the draft beers are: Harpoon Stout, John Courage Amber, J.W. Dundee's Honey Brown Lager, Stoudt's Honey Double Maibock, Young's Oatmeal Stout, Saranac Black and Tan, Watney's Cream Stout, Catamount Porter and Newcastle Brown. Drink 27 different beers for a free T-shirt. "No, you don't have to do them all in one night," Werle says.

CUB ROOM*

131 Sullivan Street (Prince)
212-677-4100

Americana Très Cool

The Cub Room is so trendy it should be bad. But it's not. There's a reason all those celebrities and trendy types – both setters and followers – take their ease here. The bar is a cozy room, a kind of subdued cool, with light woodwork, a small curved bar and an assortment of tables, upholstered armchairs and couches in front of the floor-to-ceiling windows that make for great Soho people-watching.

The six draft lines typically offer Brooklyn Lager, Sierra Nevada Pale Ale, Saranac Pilsner, Bass Ale and Amstel Light, with a seasonal such as Brooklyn Black Chocolate Stout, all served in foot-tall, heavy glasses.

The food is appealing "new American" from chef Henry Meer, formerly of Lutece: meat loaf, turkey pot pie, "plate" specials for $9-12, a good selection of soups, salads and sandwiches for $4-11, and fresh bread, fritters, scones and muffins. Beyond the bar there's an informal cafe-style dining room and another more formal one. The place is named, incidentally, after the innermost room of the old Stork Club, where only the biggest celebrities could get tables.

> Coach drivers in Olde England were expected to entertain their passengers with tall tales. Two of the coach lines were the Cock and the Bull, whose respective drivers tried to outdo each other.

CUPPING ROOM CAFE**

359 West Broadway (Broome)
212-925-2898

Casual Class with a Beer Emphasis

The entrance to the bar is on Broome, and to the dining room on West Broadway, but either door leads to good beer and people who appreciate how to cook with beer and serve it with food. This is a Soho neighborhood place with a devoted local following who often start at the small bar – six seats, four draft lines, but at least one good micro or seasonal (Brooklyn Black Chocolate Stout and Rogue Red, for example) on tap. The bottle selection is not huge, but it's thoughtful: Rodenbach Red Ale, Lindemans Framboise, Corsendonk Brown Ale, Breckenridge Oatmeal Stout, Tucher Wheat and Dark Wheat.

The beer menu is chosen by the chef, Russell Moss, with an eye toward using the beer both in his kitchen and to complement the dishes he prepares. The menu, like the beer list, is varied and innovative but not overly ambitious. Appetizers in the $7-10 range include ginger chicken wings, garlic prawns, steamed mussels and calamari in Russell's peasant sauce. Pasta for $13-16 includes fresh ravioli, linguini zangora and black pepper fettucine with either home-made chicken sausage or wild mushrooms.

There are a dozen vegetarian entrees for $8-12, along with $14-22 main courses such as baked scallops, a fish and shellfish broth with Pernod, chicken Moutard, lamb, veal and steak. Burgers and sandwiches are $8-12. The place is jammed for Sunday brunch, and kids are welcome any time.

Carol Stoudt was a kindergarten teacher in Pennsylvania before becoming an award-winning brewer.

---

d.b.a. 41
FIRST AVENUE***

41 First Avenue (2nd/3rd)
212-475-5097

Doing Business, and Beer, As It Should

Ray Deter and Dennis Zentek, the co-owners, opened d.b.a. in the autumn of 1994 with the intention of making it one of the best beer bars in the East Village. They underestimated themselves and their bar. It's quickly established itself among beer purists not only as one of the best bars in Manhattan, but one of the best in the whole country.

Don't look for pounding dance music, space-age arcade games, a pickup scene or nonstop sports TV. Instead, d.b.a. aims to provide a place for good drinking and good conversation. And while Deter and Zentek can't guarantee that patrons will solve the world's problems, they do guarantee the relaxed setting and good beer necessary to begin the process.

The draft lines, including authentic English hand pumps for cask-conditioned ale, typically offer a rotation that may feature Stoudt's Fest, Rogue Mogul Madness, Pete's, Celis White, Bateman's XXXB, Sierra Nevada Celebration, Pale Ale and Porter, along with other specials and seasonals. The owners should be applauded, by the way, for the blackboard noting the date each keg was opened.

The American beers include Anderson Valley Barney Flats Oatmeal Stout, Celis Grand Cru and Rogue Old Crustacean Barleywine. There are also seasonals from Brooklyn, Catamount, Geary's, Harpoon, New England, Samuel Smith's, Saranac and others.

From Belgium: Affligem Dobbel and Tripel; Chimay Grand Reserve Magnum; Corsendonk Brown Ale; Duvel; Liefmans Frambozen, Kriek and Goudenband; Orval Trappist, and Rodenbach Grand Cru. The Belgian ales get their own separate cooler behind the bar, set to 48-50 degrees, and their own brand glasses.

From Britain: Thomas Hardy's Ale, Young's Oatmeal Stout and Ramrod Special Bitter, and Samuel Smith's Nut Brown Ale, Oatmeal Stout, Pale Ale and Taddy Porter. From Germany, there's Ayinger Celebrator Doppel Bock and Paulaner Hefe-Weizen, and from the Czech Republic there's Pilsner Urquell.

Drafts are served in full-sized American pints, imperial pints or half-pints. Sample any three handles in six-ounce glasses for $6.

There are plans for food and a beer garden out back – a great urbanscape, with plants and tables in the middle of the brick walls and overlooking apartment buildings.

Ray Deter, a home brewer who says the good beer in her native Yorkshire is only one reason he picked an English girl to marry, has carefully screened and schooled his bar staff. Under the buy-back policy – "If you don't like it, I'll buy it back and give you whatever you want..." – new customers who ask for a Rolling Rock will end up sipping an American micro pilsner. Even committed Guinness drinkers find themselves talked into trying something new: "Hey, have you had Sierra Nevada Porter? It's got a whole different hop profile. C'mon, check out the Pacific Northwest..."

Beer conversations are encouraged, and Deter says, "We find we learn a lot from our customers." There's a library of beer books, and a bulletin board and newsletter with information about beer happenings not only at d.b.a. but elsewhere in New York. Brooklyn Brewmaster Garrett Oliver began doing tastings at d.b.a. in early 1995, and they appear to be popular enough to become fixtures.

d.b.a. has a good long bar with plenty of room for standing, and tables of different sizes, many of them attended by old pews, stretching back in the long room. The ceiling is high, the lighting indirect and the music a nice mix of blues, jazz, r 'n' b and new alternative rock. Families, even with small kids and strollers, are welcome when the place isn't too crowded. d.b.a. also has good selections of single malts, ports and tequilas.

DIVE BAR*

732 Amsterdam Avenue (96th)
212-749-4358

C'mon In, The Beer's Fine

Yes, it's a dive, and thank goodness it is. For every beer drinker who's had enough ferns, beautiful young waitpersons, unpronounceable menus and earth-tone murals, a place like the Dive Bar is a welcome refuge.

Yeah, there may be an old drunk or two, mumbling or half-asleep with his head on the bar, but that's part of the charm of a dive. This Dive also has three dozen beers, many of them good ones: Anderson Valley, Chimay, Scaldis, Duvel, Saison Dupont, Wild Boar and Samuel Smith's Taddy Porter, Oatmeal Stout and Winter Welcome. Indeed, last January there were 13 entries on the winter special blackboard.

The Dive Bar's name is justified by a smattering of scuba and other seafaring stuff on the walls, but it's perhaps more instructive that there is also a well-used dart board, three well-used TVs and a well-used pool table in the back – the real signs of a dive. Check out the souvenir T-shirts, long-sleeved.

Incidentally, the owner, Lee Seinfeld, is a deep-sea fisherman who organizes trips out of Sheepshead Bay for customers. They usually return with a hold full of fish and at least a couple of empty kegs.

Spike Lee, whose film company is based in Brooklyn, has used Brooklyn beers in his movies and served them at publicity and production parties.

DR. FINLEY'S PUBLICK HOUSE***

43 Green Street, Huntington Village
516-351-3440

Old English on Long Island

This is what happens when a family of Anglophiles who love English ales and stouts decides to open a bar and restaurant. Finley's is a good restaurant with upscale pub grub and a genteel dining area (food til 3 a.m.), but its real treasure is the tap room and 32 draft lines.

Some of the draft choices from England include Bass, Fuller's ESB, Newcastle Brown, Watneys Cream Stout, Woodpecker Cider, Whitbread and Young's Oatmeal Stout. From Germany: Paulaner Hefe-Weizen and Salvator, Spaten and Warsteiner. The American micros on offer include brews from Anchor, Catamount, Harpoon, Pete's and Samuel Adams.

In bottles, there's a choice of dozens more. The Belgian list alone includes: Affligem Dobbel and Tripel; Blanches de Bruges; Boon Gueuze, Kriek, Faro and Framboise; Chimay Rouge, Cinq Cents and Grand Reserve; Corsendonk Brown; Dent-ergems Wit; Duvel; Hoegaarden; Gouden Carolus; Kwak; Liefmans Goudenband, Frambozen and Kriek; Lindemans Peche, Framboise and Kriek; Orval Trappist; Rodenbach Red; St. Sixtus; Scaldis; Saison Dupont, and Witkap Singel.

Some of the rarer American micro bottles include Abita Turbodog, Anderson Valley, Olde Heurich, Old Peconic, Pike Place, Rogue Old Crustacean Barleywine, Rogue Shakespeare Stout and Telluride.

"I believe in variety. People should be able to get whatever good beer they want," says Shannon Finley, who used to work with his older brother D.R. in Eerie Entertainment Inc., the pub group in the city (Jekyll and Hyde, Jack the Ripper, Slaughtered Lamb), before opening this place with his father, a retired sea captain who became a dentist before finding his true calling as a publican.

One of the best things about Finley's is the series of outdoor decks in the big beer garden, which includes a clam bar and barbecue pit. One of the worst, but least surprising, things about Finley's is the long line of people waiting to get in on a Friday or Saturday night. Go early and stay late.

DORAL ARROWWOOD*

Anderson Hill Road, Rye Brook
914-939-5500

Resorting to Good Beer

One of the best hotel resorts in the New York suburbs, Arrowwood has long been a destination for golfers. Whether out on the terrace or at the tables overlooking the swimming pool, it's defnitely a place for good beer. The selection includes Catamount Porter, Dock Street Amber, Lindemans Framboise, New England Amber, Rodenbach Red Ale and, on draft, Sierra Nevada Pale Ale.

EAST SIDE ALE HOUSE***

961 Second Avenue (51st)
212-752-3615

Step Up to the Top Shelf

The only bad thing about the East Side Ale House is that it's up one flight, on top of a pizza joint. But if that's the worst thing you can say about a bar, it must be pretty good. The East Side Ale House is not just pretty good. This is one of the best bars in New York City.

Opened in July 1994 by ownership and management with a long history in the beer business, the East Side Ale House quickly became a regular haunt in Midtown for beer lovers, both locals and out-of-towners staying at the many hotels in the area. Any concierge who is asked about places to get good beer and doesn't mention the East Side Ale House shouldn't get a tip.

In terms of looks, the East Side Ale House is functional rather than spectacular. The L-shaped bar is good-sized, and there are tables and stools, too. That's fine; the goal was to set up a traditional tavern or ale house, and that's what this is. Food is limited to burgers, sandwiches, wings – and pizza, of course.

The printed beer menu, which includes a brief description of the brewing process on the back, lists close to five dozen American microbrews and good imports, but there are always a few specials and seasonals that aren't on the list. Don't be discouraged if they've run out of your first choice; the beer is deliberately ordered in small quantities to guarantee freshness, so occasional gaps in the menu are understandable.

The bartenders are trained not only to know the beers they sell, but to understand the brewing processes behind the beer. That's one of the reasons that so many do-it-yourself beerfolk call the East Side Ale House their home away from home brewing.

There are 20 draft lines, usually broken down into 12-15 micros and 5-8 imports. Examples: Dock Street Amber, Harpoon IPA, Catamount Amber, Saranac Pale Ale, Pilsner Urquell, Watney's Red Barrel, John Courage Amber.

The American micros in bottles are fairly represented by this cross section: Breckenridge Ale; Catamount Porter; Geary's Pale Ale; Grant's Imperial Stout and Scottish Ale; Harpoon Ale; New England Light Lager and Stock Ale; Rogue Ale; Samuel Adams Honey Porter; Saranac Pale Ale; Telluride, and Wild Boar Amber.

Some typical fall/winter seasonals: Brooklyn Black Chocolate Stout, Hacker-Pschorr Oktoberfest, Spaten Oktoberfest, Samuel Adams' Oktoberfest, Buffalo Bill's Pumpkin Ale, Catamount Christmas Ale, Grant's Spiced Ale,

Saranac Season's Best and Sierra Nevada Celebration Ale.

Besides the beer, the East Side Ale House lists more than 20 single malt scotches, including Knockando, Talisker, Laphroaig, Cragganmore and Bunnahabhain, and several fine bourbons and mashes, including Maker's Mark VIP, Gentleman Jack and Wild Turkey Rare Breed.

FIREHOUSE*

522 Columbus Avenue (85th)
212-595-3139

Home of the Dalmation Logo

Firehouse is a nice little neighborhood bar-restaurant that has become inordinately famous because of its hats, T-shirts, sweatshirts, jackets, watches and other stuff depicting Dalmations – gear that is particularly trendy among the famous and wannabe's of the Upper West Side. While two of the four draft lines are wasted except for Sam Adams, most of the 30-some bottled beers are from microbreweries, including Pete's, Saranac, Cave Creek, Wit and Harpoon.

This is yet another of the many places where the management claims Matt Dillon is a semi-regular or at least makes occasional appearances. They cast all their celebrity claims in doubt, however, by implying that Howard Stern drops in every now and then; even the radio satirist's casual listeners know he doesn't drink and hates to hang out except in bars where the strippers know him. Firehouse food includes the usual lineup of snacks, pizza and burgers, with maybe a little more chili and hot sauce than most, and all for under $8. There's a decent children's menu.

Prohibition began on Jan. 16, 1920

FIRST**

87 First Avenue (5th/6th)
212-674-3823

Late-Night, Inner-City Flavor

Chef and owner Sam DeMarco, a veteran of upscale, uptown hotel kitchens, opened this place in the summer of 1994 and found immediate success with his creative, cross-cultural menu that changes with the seasons.

The black and chrome decor is stylish but not fancy, and the 12-stool bar is a good staging area before dinner, which is served until 2 a.m. weeknights and 3 a.m. Thursday through Saturday nights. People in tuxedos and evening gowns can sit next to people in jeans and T-shirts.

First isn't a beer-drinking place, but DeMarco really cares about making sure the right beers are available for his food. He typically has a pale ale, a light and a pilsner on draft, and always has a few seasonals – Lindemans Peche and wheats are summer favorites – among the handful of good bottles. A recent menu had Sierra Nevada Porter and Paulaner Pilsner on draft, along with bottles of Samuel Smith's Nut Brown Ale, Belle-Vue Kriek and Rogue Mogul.

The food draws on the many ethnic influences, from Caribbean to Calcutta, in the downtown area. A few seasonal highlights: in summer, crab cakes with mango relish; in autumn, seafood chili with shrimp jack cheese quesadilla; in winter, hanger steak and pork chops; in spring, maple mustard glazed salmon. And no less than *Gourmet* magazine has proclaimed First's squid dishes the best in town, especially the squid rings with salad. Appetizers are generally $6-9, sandwiches (meat loaf, calzone, roast turkey dip) around $10, and entrees average around $15.

It's a sign of DeMarco's success that so many Uptowners, particularly other chefs, come down to his restaurant, especially in the wee hours after finishing their own shifts and on winter Sunday nights when he does a pig roast.

FOFFÉ*

155 Montague Street (Clinton/Henry),
Brooklyn
718-875-3455

Upstairs, Downstairs

Half a flight down is an Italian restaurant with
brick walls, utilitarian tables and chairs and
Sinatra on the juke. It's inviting. One flight up is
a funky little bar with upholstered chairs and
sofas and oriental rugs that look like they've
been salvaged from a wealthy aunt's attic. It's
very inviting.

Upstairs, there's live jazz on weekends and a
good lineup of bottled beer, including Catamount
Porter, Chimay Grand Reserve, Duvel, Edelweiss, Grant's, Lindemans, Moinette Blonde,
Pike Place, Rogue, Scaldis and Stoudt's. There
are nine draft lines but, unhappily, micros are
under-represented on the tap handles. The bar
menu includes burgers, pizza and finger food
such as skins, sweet potato fries, wings, baked
clams, chicken fingers and mozzarella sticks.

FRANK'S RESTAURANT*

85 Tenth Avenue (15th)
212-243-1349

Classic Italian Steakhouse

After decades at the far west end of 14th Street in
the old meat-packing district, Frank's moved in
early 1995 to its fine new space in the Manhattan
Industrial Center. Its many loyal customers were
quick to follow around the corner, and were
rewarded to find draft beer in the new Frank's,
including Brooklyn Lager. Jimmy Molinari,
whose family owns the place, also stocks some
fine French and Belgian country ales – perfect
for washing down a thick rare one.

FRAUNCES TAVERN

54 Pearl Street (Broad)
212-269-0144

Downtown Revolutionary Landmark

With its upstairs museum and a couple centuries' worth of military history on the walls, it's hard to forget that Fraunces has been a popular tavern since 1762. Its namesake, one of the leaders among the many black patriots in the Colonies, is remembered in history for giving aid and comfort (and fortifying ale) to the Sons of Liberty. In 1783, George Washington chose Fraunces as the place to throw a farewell dinner for his officers at the end of the Revolutionary War.

Today's Fraunces is popular with both tourists and downtown workers. There's a Georgian-style formal dining room, and the bar features a menu of burgers, sandwiches and salad for $6-16, along with daily specials on oysters. The beer includes Dinkel Acker and Whitbread Ale, but the best bet is Fraunces' own brand, Tavern Keeper Ale, which is actually Brooklyn Brown.

Fraunces at times has specials on beer, such as a draft for a mere penny. Those who are lucky enough to be on the premises are advised not to be greedy – it's bad form – and to make sure the bartenders get a tip of at least $2 per penny beer. This is, after all, still the Financial District.

There was a time in Scotland when the common medical treatment for a dog bite was to pluck a few hairs from the offending dog and place them on the wound. Hence "hair of the dog" became an expression for having a drink to ease a hangover.

FRIEND OF A FARMER*

77 Irving Place (18th/19th)
212-477-2188

"Made of Warmth and Wood"

This cozy Gramercy Park restaurant strives to be a "country cafe" in Manhattan – and carries it off reasonably well. The plank floors, wood beams, flower-print wallpaper and rustic decorations make a fine setting for a menu that lists spinach meatloaf, ribs, steak and several styles of chicken. Most entrees, including a variety of vegetarian offerings, are in the $12-15 range. The bakery menu is something special, with several types of fresh bread, muffins, cakes, pies and brownies.

The beer list has a nice mix of American micros, including Brooklyn Lager, Pike Place Lager, Catamount Porter and Grant's Celtic Ale. There's a fireplace inside in winter and tables on the sidewalk the rest of the year.

GOTHAM BAR AND GRILL**

12 East 12th Street (5th Ave)
212-620-4030

Batman Would Like It; Bruce Wayne, Too

This is not the sort of the place the phrase "bar and grill" automatically brings to mind. The Gotham Bar and Grill is one of the most widely- and well-reviewed restaurants in town. It is, in a word, elegant, with a marble bar, pale pink and green motif, music that slides easily from medieval chants to plaintive sax, and a menu that features venison, squab and pheasant for around $30. Starters, at about half the price, might be wild game terrine, duck breast or butternut squash risotto.

The beer list fits with the rest of the program – first class all the way. The actual beer menu is pasted on a gilded card and lists 18 brews, a few of them run-of-the-mill domestics. Most, however, are very good, including: Pinkus Ur Pils; Sierra Nevada Pale Ale; Samuel Smith's Pale Ale, Nut Brown Ale and Taddy Porter; Chimay Rouge, and Paulaner Hefe-Weizen.

No matter what your budget, every now and then it's extravagantly healthy, or perhaps healthily extravagant, to sit down in a place that doesn't have sawdust on the floor or graffiti in the bathroom and exercise the right to pay $6 or more for a bottle of beer. When that time comes, this is a great place to do it.

GRAMERCY TAVERN**

42 East 20th Street (B'way/Park)
212-477-0777

Ambitious American, Including Micros

A spacious, tony restaurant, Gramercy Tavern opened in the summer of 1994 with a blaze of publicity for its frank aspirations to become a "great" restaurant…whatever that is. There's obviously money – and good taste – behind it, from the slick press package to the eye-pleasing decor. The airy front bar, the "tavern" area, offers a relaxed, almost country-inn look with its Windsor chairs, oriental rugs and tables that aren't jammed together. The slightly cheaper tavern menu is regarded as one of the best opportunities in Manhattan to eat expensive dishes at not-quite-so-expensive prices.

In the other two, more formal and more pricey dining rooms, the food includes specialties such as: seared tuna with white beans, lemon and arugula; roast rabbit with black olives and sherry vinegar, and lobster and artichoke salad. One of the best food features is the selection of cheese – something that Americans gradually are learning to appreciate after the main course.

There are a laudable eight American micros on draft, with early 1995 prices starting at $5.25 for a pint or $2.25 for a 5-ounce "taste." The winter list included Brooklyn Lager (the kitchen staff's year-round favorite), Pete's Wicked Lager, Anchor Steam, Rogue Red, Harpoon IPA, New England Oatmeal Stout, Stoudt's Double Honey Maibock, Sierra Nevada Celebration and Sunday River Black Bear Porter. Of these, if you haven't tried Stoudt's Bock, it's recommended.

Incidentally, the drinks menu boasts that the draft beer is served "on tap in a frosted mug," so if you don't want an icy glass, make sure to ask the bartender to hold the frost.

The bottled beers offer some fine imports, mostly in large-size bottles suitable for sharing: Affligem Dobbel, Paulaner Hefe-Weizen, Boon Kriek, Duvel Ale, and Samuel Smith's Nut Brown Ale and Winter Welcome.

GRANGE HALL*

50 Commerce Street (Barrow)
212-924-5246

A West Village Neighborhood Restaurant

Tucked away in a charming little corner of the Village, convenient for the Cherry Lane Theatre, this is a friendly restaurant with reasonable prices: $25 and under for dinner, for example, including a microbrew or two from the cheerful bar adjacent the dining room. On tap on a Friday night, when the bar was crowded with the Village 20s-to-30s crowd: Brooklyn Black Chocolate Stout, Weinhard's Red and Boylan's birch beer.

Lunch includes sandwich plates for under $7, but the place closes in the late afternoon until 5:30 p.m. Staples are fish, poultry, meat and pasta dishes. Meals can be ordered "simple," for a reduced price, or "complete," with soup and salad. A good place to eat with kids. For you Midwesterners' bemusement, *Zagat* describes Grange Hall as having a "Wisconsin atmosphere" – whatever that means ...

HENRY'S END**

44 Henry Street (Cranberry), Brooklyn
718-834-1776

Classy Dining in the Heights

Henry's End is not a fancy place in terms of requiring ties and jackets; jeans are fine, too. But the menu is worthy of many better-known, higher-priced "new American" restaurants on the other side of the East River. Consider that the menu typically lists three different duck dishes – raspberry, honey and ginger, wild mushroom and lingonberry – even when the cafe isn't having its annual winter gamefest.

The 50-seat restaurant is nearly always crowded for dinner (unfortunately, lunch is not served) and there are many regulars, both from Brooklyn and, particularly on weekends, from Manhattan. It's not unusual for a table to order the food and tell the waiter or the manager to pick the beer for each course. On one recent evening, a party of four was started with Celis White, went to Sierra Pale, then Whitbread Ale and Duvel with the main course, followed by a pre-dessert Kriek.

A few of the many other beers on the robust list include John Courage, Ayinger Celebrator, Chimay Rouge, Orval Trappist Ale, Duvel, Old Peculier, Mackeson Stout, Thomas Hardy, Pinkus Ur Weizen, Harpoon and Anderson Valley Barney Flats Oatmeal Stout.

This restaurant is a real find, the kind of low-profile place that New Yorkers love to discover. If you're visiting from out of town, impress your New York friends by taking them here. It's one of those rare places that somehow creates an atmosphere blending relaxation with the excitement of very good food.

The Scots celebrate Burns Night on the 25th of January.

HI LIFE BAR AND GRILL*

477 Amsterdam Avenue (83rd)
212-282-7199

Been There, Drank That, Got the Hat

The sister, or maybe cousin, of the Hi Life
Lounge on the Upper East Side, this Upper West
Side rendition reflects the differences between
the two sides of town. In the space that was once
The Forest and the Sea, a Thai restaurant pioneer on Amsterdam Avenue back in the early
'80s wave of gentrification, the Hi Life Bar and
Grill is a little more worn and a little less formal,
with a scarred wooden bar, tin sheeting on the
walls, painted brick and old photos of neighborhood athletes and celebrities.

The reviews in the windows are positive and
emphasize the large portions of food. The ten
draft lines offer Bass, Guinness, Pilsner Urquell,
Anchor Steam, Saranac Gold and Brooklyn
Lager. Check out the baseball caps, which look
like Yankees' hats except the Y is a martini glass.

HI LIFE LOUNGE*

1340 First Avenue (72nd)
212-249-3600

Cocktails, Anyone?

The Hi Life Lounge is something of a throwback
to the era when the martini reigned supreme.
Black and silver with art deco accents, it has the
feel of an old 1950s cocktail lounge, except with
grilled, stir-fry and vegetarian dishes, in a choice
of big or small bowls or platters, depending on
your appetite and budget. The beer list is also
very 1990s, including Rogue, Saranac and other
micros. Don't be surprised, as out-of-towners can
be, at walking into the bar on a weekday afternoon and being advised that the place has closed
suddenly for an hour or so because the bartender needs to restock from the basement.

HORSEFEATHERS*

94 N. Broadway (Route 9), Tarrytown
914-631-6606

Put a Head on That

Horsefeathers, in a small strip of storefronts in downtown Tarrytown, is the place to stop to eat and have a beer while exploring Washington Irving country. Russ and Suzanne Rodgers, who opened Horsefeathers in the early 1980s, have made the place relaxing and interesting, with good quotes from famous people on the wall, and a good mix of standard and vegetarian food that Rip Van Winkle would have been happy to wake up to. Kids are welcome, and can entertain themselves with Trivial Pursuit cards on the tables.

If Ichabod Crane were alive today, he'd probably be a beer weenie hanging out at Horsefeathers. His choices: Ayinger Celebrator, Brasseurs, Catamount Amber and Porter, Corsendonk Brown, Grant's Imperial Stout, Pike Place Pale Ale, Saranac Black and Tan, and Samuel Smith's Lager, Nut Brown Ale, Oatmeal Stout and Pale Ale.

Leading up to Halloween, the mix of Sleepy Hollow lore and Oktoberfest beer specials make Horsefeathers a popular stop for people who head north for leaf-looking in the Hudson Valley.

HURRICANE ISLAND*

1303 Third Avenue (74th/75th)
212-717-6600

Cajun-Caribbean and Party Time

With its spicy food, youngish crowd and party-time feel, this seafood restaurant is a reminder of what a playground the Upper East Side can be for the many in their 20s and 30s who come to New York to find out if they really can make it anywhere. Lobster, flown in privately from Maine, is a specialty here.

More could be done with the draft lines – Sierra Nevada was the sole micro on tap on a recent visit – but the 30-some bottled beers include a number of very good brands, notably Thomas Hardy's, Celis, Samuel Smith's, Catamount, Pilsner Urquell and Geary's. The long bar at the entrance has 18 seats, and every one of them is a good spot to order one of those labels and observe the alphabet soup of NYC life: Generation Xers meet each other, fall in love, get married and become DINKs (dual income, no kids), and ultimately move to the suburbs and become SITCOMs (single income, two children, outrageous mortgage).

IRIDIUM*

44 West 63rd Street (Columbus)
212-246-3745

Surreal, But the Beer and Jazz Are Real

The dictionary defines iridium alternately as a rainbow, or as a chemical element with a boiling point of 4,800 degrees Centigrade. The dictionary needs another entry to cover this upscale restaurant and jazz club opposite Lincoln Center.

With Sierra Nevada on tap and a good collection of micros and imports in bottles, Iridium is an irregularly shaped, quirkily decorated but thoroughly likeable place – a good complement to the elegant dining of nearby Picholine. Iridium is plush and green and purple, and the mushroom-like stools help make the upstairs bar and restaurant look like something out of *Alice Through the Looking Glass*. The downstairs nightly jazz rooms feature a few big names, but owners Ken and Ron Sturm – whose mother Ellen is a former Miss New York and now owns Ellen's Stardust Diner – mostly bring in young up-and-comers.

Iridium is the definitive place for mainstream jazz, decent food and good beer in and around Lincoln Center. You could look it up.

JACK THE RIPPER PUB**

228 West 4th Street (W. 10th)
212-627-5225

Authentic Greenwich – On Hudson

The "straightest" of the Eerie Entertainment Inc., pubs (Slaughtered Lamb and the two Jekyll and Hydes play up the ghoulish angle), the Jack the Ripper sticks to its 1970s-80s English pub theme a bit too well at times. The beer selection is great, the Fine Young Cannibals pound out on the sound system and the wait staff is friendly but not always helpful or flexible.

For any serious beer drinker, however, Jack's can be a happy experience. Along with Fullers, Murphys and four other beers on draft, the bottle selection includes the Sierra Nevada range, Pete's, Paulaner, Lindemans Framboise, Duvel, Corsendonk and an all-star lineup from England: Double Diamond, Courage, Mackesons Stout, Newcastle Brown, Old Peculier, Royal Oak, five different Samuel Smith's brews, Young's London Special Bitter and Oatmeal Stout, and Thomas Hardy's from the West Country.

The Jack the Ripper Pub is worth a stop to fill in some of the blank spots on your lifetime beer dance card, or for a taste of a Covent Garden local without the overnight flight to London.

JAKE'S DILEMMA**

430 Amsterdam Avenue (80th/81st)
212-580-0556

Serving Your Foosball and Beer Needs

There is no Jake, but the dilemma is real: what to choose from 50-plus bottled beers and 10 drafts. This is a straightforward Upper West Side beer bar with a healthy emphasis on American micros. The music gets loud at night, the only food is popcorn or peanuts, and the place is a nationally-sanctioned Foosball site…which helps explain the shouts of agony or exultation from the guys (and gals) crowded around the tables.

Jake's offers Brooklyn Lager, Catamount Porter, Harpoon IPA and Sierra Nevada Pale Ale on tap, along with seasonals. The bottles include Catamount Amber, Celis White, Geary's Ale, and Saranac Golden Pilsner and Pale Ale.

Jake's, which opened in October 1994 with a new wooden floor and newly-exposed brick, also has a new draft system that uses steel rather than PVC lines, which helps keep the beer cold. The bartenders are knowledgeable and happy to talk beer or about their own experiences as homebrewers or working in microbreweries. The managers are considering a program of micro tastings.

The crowd is typically Upper West Side, and more singles-oriented than couples. Things get pretty packed around 10 o'clock most evenings, so go before or after that if you want a seat at the bar or one of the three booths.

JAMES BAY BREWING CO.

154 W. Broadway, Port Jefferson
516-928-2525

Brewing on the Bay

Jeff Smith was an airline pilot who got into good beer during layovers on the West Coast. When he got a chance for early retirement, he threw himself into a serious brewing education and rounded up some buddies from the local yacht club to help raise money. Together they opened this brewpub and restaurant on the harbor in Port Jefferson in the summer of 1994. The place was an immediate success, both financially and also beer-wise.

Perhaps the best thing about Smith and his brewing, however, is that he isn't sitting on his laurels or, like some other new East Coast brewpub brewers, believing his press clippings. Just because the place is making money doesn't mean the beer is perfect. "We've been taking some of the beer to festivals, and getting good results," Smith says. "Don't get me wrong. I think we're making some wonderful beer now. But I don't think we're really up to West Coast standards yet."

He reckons that as his clientele – not as sophisticated as the drinkers who populate the more mature brewpub scene in the West – become more eager to wean themselves away from light lagers, the beer he crafts at James Bay will become more sophisticated, too. Smith credits much of his success to the meticulous mind of his assistant, Ray Murphy, a local microbiologist whose knowledge of yeast made him a legend in Long Island homebrewing circles. The first time Murphy came in with his own special liquid yeast, he brought in a boom box playing German oom-pah music to get in the mood for brewing.

A typical sampler at James Bay includes a Kolsch that serves as a "starter" for craft beer neophytes, a Pale Ale that stands as the pub's flagship brew, a nice Pumpkin Ale, a Winter Warmer, a respectable Porter and an especially good ESB.

Overlooking the harbor where the ferry lands from Bridgeport, Conn., the James Bay brewpub is a big place, with a large downstairs bar and a more formal upstairs restaurant. The bar menu includes burgers, chili and a selection of dishes made with beer. The entrees upstairs range up to $20.

The place is crowded, especially on weekends and especially in summer, when the outdoor deck is the place to be.

> **"The best audience is intelligent, well-educated and a little bit drunk."**
> **Alben W. Barkley**

JEKYLL AND HYDE CLUB**

1409 Sixth Avenue (57th/58th)
212-541-9532

Is This What Robert Louis Stevenson Had In Mind?

Back when the Yankees were dominating baseball, almost every post-game was a celebration, a reason to go out on the town. DiMaggio, Mantle, Ford, Martin – hey, where we going tonight? One night, somebody invited Yogi Berra to the hottest new watering hole.

"Nahh," Berra said. "Nobody goes there. It's always too crowded."

That's how some – not many, admittedly – good beer drinkers feel about the new uptown Jekyll and Hyde Club, the biggest and newest in the Eerie Entertainment Inc., pub chain (also the Slaughtered Lamb, Jack the Ripper and Jekyll and Hyde pubs, all in Greenwich Village). Ever since the place opened in January 1995 amid great fanfare, as the latest in a line of 57th Street show-biz emporia including the Hard Rock Cafe and Planet Hollywood, it's been known that there's a world-class beer list behind that imposing Temple of Doom facade. But only drinkers willing to wait behind the ropes on Sixth Avenue can get to it.

One eager visitor tried to get in several times, at different times of day or night. Even at four o'clock on a weekday afternoon, however, there was a line of at least a dozen people. Pleading that he just wanted to stand by the bar and have one drink cut no ice with the burly but polite doorman in his snakeboots, jodhpurs, leather jacket and Indiana Jones hat.

Perhaps as more areas of the restaurant open – expansion is rumored to be under way – the lines will disappear. At any rate, this would-be visitor decided not to pull rank with his press card, or make an appointment for special treatment because he was working on a guide book. Instead he took to telephoning to find out the length of the wait – no reservations are taken – and learned that there's more waiting inside. "Twenty-five minutes on the sidewalk, 15 minutes inside," was the phone receptionist's typical response on a midweek mid-evening.

Once inside, according to press reports and comments of those who've survived the queue, the Jekyll and Hyde Club is worth the wait. Prices for food and beer are high, as expected, but the entertainment – sinking bar stools, eyes in paintings that follow you, 20 actors playing a variety of interactive roles with customers – is good for lots of laughs. As for the beer, credit must go to D.R. Finley, the entrepreneur who is taking "restaurtainment" to new heights. As with his earlier bars, Finley has blessed the new Jekyll with an impressive beer menu (listed with the other Eerie pubs) that is all the more remarkable because the odds are that people would still wait 40 minutes to get in even if the only beer on offer was the kind that sponsors NFL games.

Lift a beer to good old D.R. – if and when you get in. But don't expect to see Yogi there.

JEKYLL AND HYDE PUB**

91 Seventh Avenue South (Barrow/Grove)
212-989-7701

Forget About Having a 'Quiet' Beer

This is the older, downtown version of the trendy uptown bar of the same name, both (along with Jack the Ripper and the Slaughtered Lamb) part of entrepreneur and beer lover D.R. Finley's Eerie Entertainment Inc., pub chain. The beer list is tremendous, but Jekyll uptown or down is not to everybody's taste. Yes, you can order a Castelain or Dentergems or Liefmans Goudenband (some say it's the world's best brown ale) or a Boon Gueuze or a Blanche de Bruges – that's not even half of the list from Belgium – but you may have to drink it amid loud music ("The Monster Mash," for example), old horror movies, and actors dressed as mad scientists or explorers intent on making customers part of the entertainment.

Not to be a curmudgeon, this place and all the other Eerie pubs can be a lot of fun, if you're in the mood. A lot of people are always in the mood, and regard the Jekyll and Hyde Pub as a great night out – even though they may be rueful about the prices. It's worth finding a comfortable seat under the T-rex skull, picking out a beer (pints and yards are available) and succumbing to the scene.

Unfortunately, the 20-plus draft beers are not as distinguished as the bottle selection. There are more than 200 bottles, and some are difficult to find even in New York. Brand names from Europe include Ayinger, Hacker-Pschorr, Paulaner, Wurzburger, Edelweiss, Bateman's, Royal Oak, Samuel Smith's, Thomas Hardy's and Traquair.

American micros include Catamount, Celis, Grant's, Harpoon, Pete's, Samuel Adams, Saranac, Sierra Nevada, Telluride and Wit. Beers from at least three continents represented on Jekyll and Hyde's list weren't mentioned here because they aren't that good.

The Jekyll and Hyde Pub is a great place to go with a bunch of people who are up for anything and like good beer. Please, please, please, if you do go – don't let anyone in you party order a beer advertised on American television. It would be a wasted opportunity.

Only six Trappist monasteries still produce beer. In Holland: Trappe. In Belgium: Rochefort, Chimay, St. Sixtus, Orval and Westmalle. Abbey ales are made in the Trappist style, but not at monasteries.

JIMMY ARMSTRONG'S SALOON**

875 Tenth Avenue (57th)
212-581-0606

Beer Heaven in Hell's Kitchen

Roger Protz, a leader of Britain's Campaign for Real Ale, calls Armstrong's his favorite bar in Manhattan. Anyone who knows anything about CAMRA realizes that Roger's favorite is really the bar he's in at the moment, or the one he's going to next. But in this case, his praise is not only heartfelt, but deserved. There is a real Jimmy Armstrong (he's a big guy who looks a bit like Santa) and he's made this a real saloon.

Armstrong's is a classic New York neighborhood joint set on a corner of Hell's Kitchen, the tough area that spawned so many actors and comedians in the first half of this century. The area was also the setting for Leonard Bernstein's operatic *West Side Story*, arguably the greatest American musical.

But the reason to go to Armstrong's is not old entertainment history. The place is a landmark for its ambiance, its conviviality, its food and, especially in recent years, its beer. The beer menu typically includes a dozen drafts, such as Young's Oatmeal Stout, Rogue Mogul Madness, Paulaner Oktoberfest, Brooklyn Brown, Weinhard Red and Stoudt's Gold. There are only a few bottled beers, but they're well-chosen imports and micros, too. There are also rotating seasonals and specials.

With its dark polished wood, leaded glass, tasteful paintings and intricate carvings and sculpture, Armstrong's presents a comforting, welcoming atmosphere. The bar area is narrow, but easily overflows to the tables in the entryway or the small dining area. Food, served anywhere in the place, is an intriguing combination of Mediterranean and Caribbean styles: Haitian-style smoked cod; Cuban blood sausage; sardine sandwiches; Cuban sandwiches; chorizo and extra-sharp cheddar, and ceviche. There are also standards such as pork chops, shell steak and burgers. Nothing's more than $15, and a lot is closer to $5, making this a reasonable place for lunch or dinner. Free bar snacks include crispy corn chips with a salsa sauce; like many of the bar snacks, they're spicy enough to stand up to the strong and flavorful beers served here.

JOHNNEY'S FISH GRILL*

250 Vesey Street (World Financial Center)
212-385-0333

Fat Cats and Lean Catfish

It's generally easy to hate those big artificial-looking bar-restaurants that are supposed to bring some life to atrium architecture. Johnney's, with its checked tablecloths and made-to-look-old fishing paraphernalia, fits that category. But this is a place that's hard to hate and easy to like.

Set amid the glitz and glass of the World Financial Center, on the Hudson River edge of the money district, Johnney's is a favorite lunch place for seafood fans from all over downtown, and a favorite after-work stop for good beer fans, especially those taking the ferry across to Hoboken. Entrees such as crab cakes and a variety of grilled, blackened and sauteed seafood are generally under $20, and the raw bar offers oyster specials for under $1 apiece. There's a small collection of micros, including Sierra Nevada and Brooklyn, to help wash them down. A recommended order: a dozen bluepoints and either a Sierra Nevada Pale Ale draft or a Brooklyn Lager bottle or, preferably, one after the other.

> **Reinheitsgebot, the German beer purity law, dates back to 1516 in Bavaria.**

JOSIE'S**

344 Amsterdam Avenue (74th)
212-769-1212

Yes, Beer is Good for You

If beer wasn't good for you, Josie's wouldn't sell it. This restaurant is perhaps New York's boldest attempt to prove that a good restaurant – from setting to presentation to food to service – can also be health-oriented.

There are three draft lines and a fine but not large selection of micros and imports – all craft-brewed, with only natural ingredients, of course – including Dock Street Bohemian Pils, Pike Place Lager, Rogue Red Ale, Sierra Nevada Pale Ale, Paulaner Thomas Brau and Stoudt's Abbey, Bock and Export Gold.

There's a good beer menu with descriptions such as this one for Celis White: "Divinely complex, the refreshing taste of wheaty tartness leans against the novel use of curacao orange peel and coriander. Uplifting and exciting."

The bar offers nearly as many fresh juices as beers, and the menu boasts entrees such as sweet potato ravioli, cornmeal-coated Mississippi catfish, free-range chicken, organic beef, and marinated Portobello mushroom fajitas with tomato avocado salsa and a whole-wheat tortilla.

Josie's attracts a fair number of show business and other celebrity types, partly because of the menu and partly because one of the co-owners is Rob Morrow, who starred in the television series "Northern Exposure" and in the film *Quiz Show*.

In Victorian London, someone who had too much to drink was said to be "drunk as blazes," in reference to the devil.

JULES BISTRO*

65 St. Marks Place (1st/2nd Aves)
212-477-5560

Authentic French Fare in
the East Village

On and around St. Marks Place is where the trendy people who live in Greenwich Village come when they want to leave the neighborhood but still be trendy. Convenient for the funky shops, theater and movies, Jules Bistro is a relaxed and very French restaurant with couscous, steak frites and other typical menu entries in the $10-16 range. Note: cash only, no credit cards.

There are about a dozen bottled beers, including St. Amand French Country Ale, Jenlain and Sierra Nevada. The place becomes more Parisian, if that's possible, on Friday and Saturday nights when there's live jazz.

KIN KHAO*

171 Spring Street (W. B'way/Thompson)
212-966-3939

Adventuresome Asian

Asian restaurants aren't often known for their beer, but Soho's Kin Khao is making a worthy effort to serve microbrews that complement its flavorful satay, seafood and other dishes prepared with ginger, chilies and curries. Entrees are in the $10-18 range.

Kin Khao has a few bottled beers, but there's probably no reason to look beyond the front bar and the three draft lines featuring Brooklyn Brown, Saranac Golden Pilsner and Sierra Nevada Pale Ale. They're all good matches for the spicy stuff.

Bars and Restaurants

KINSALE TAVERN***

1672 Third Avenue (93rd-94th)
212-348-4370

Irish, But Good Beer

For people who like Irish pubs – and who does-
n't, at least now and then? – there's good news
and bad news in New York. The good news is
that the city has more bars with Irish names,
Irish themes and Irish bartenders than any place
this side of the Dingle peninsula. They are particularly thick on the ground on Third Avenue in
Manhattan. The bad news is that very few of
them, on Third Avenue or anywhere else, have
much of a selection of good beer.

True, many pour Guinness, Murphy's and/or
Harp – all fine beers, usually on draft and served
in straight pint glasses. But beyond that there's
not much choice save for big-name American
domestics in all their light, ice and "genuine"
nonflavors. The happy exception is Kinsale
Tavern, which manages to combine the best of
an authentic Irish pub's casual friendliness (people are in there drinking at 8 a.m.) with the best
of a good American neighborhood tavern's food,
service and, of course, quality beer.

The blackboards on the wall list more than
100 beers, broken down by style: three brown
ales, for example, four porters and five wheats.
The draft lines include Sierra Nevada, Anchor
Steam Liberty, Double Diamond and other
micros and imports. Pints are $4 or less and a 10-
ounce glass is $2.25. Kinsale Tavern also recent-
ly added 15 Belgian beers, giving it one of the
best-rounded beer lists in the city. While Kinsale
Tavern does draw its share of aficionados just for
the beer, it's kind of nice that the place is more of
a neighborhood eatery and watering hole that
also happens to serve a lot of very good beer.
Bars such as Kinsale Tavern – everything's like
before, except the beer list has steadily gotten

better and better – are going to become more common in New York and elsewhere.

Kinsale Tavern's dark green walls and New York saloon decor are nothing special. There are 20 stools at the bar, but room for twice as many to stand behind the stools, and they do. Pub grub is available at the tables along the wall and in back, including chicken pot pie, crab cakes, salmon, lamb chops and an Irish mixed grill, all for under $10. The TVs don't dominate like in some sports bars, but when a big event is on this is serious male bonding territory.

KNITTING FACTORY**

74 Leonard Street (Church)
212-219-3055

Alternative Performance Space

This three-story club includes two performance spaces for the nightly jazz, poetry, dance, independent film, theater and multi-media. Michael Dorf, the owner, describes himself as "a guy from Wisconsin" who didn't know the club scene was dead when he and some friends came to New York a few years ago and began the Knitting Factory as a laboratory for cultural and artistic experiments and cross-pollination.

Music, much of it from Europe, dominates the Knitting Factory lineup. Recent acts include: the Jazz Passengers, James "Blood" Ulmer, Henry Threadgill, John Zorn's Cobra, They Might Be Giants, the Alloy Orchestra, Arto Lindsay, Wayne Horvitz, Bill Frisell, World Saxophone Quartet, Pharoah Sanders, Don Byron, Joe Lovano, Bartokking Heads, Human Feel – a lineup ranging from klezmer to classical to new rock.

With the kind of crowd drawn by those acts, it's no wonder the Wisconsin guys decided that they needed beer to match. Their downstairs Tap Room, with 18 draft lines, serves as much variety as the performances, including many micros such as New York Harbor, Harpoon, Brooklyn, Sierra Nevada, Pete's, New Amsterdam, Dock Street, Stoudt's, New England and Saranac.

The place retains much of its old factory feel, but there are some nice touches such as the overstuffed furniture in the Tap Room downstairs, and the pastel murals in the coffee house near the street entrance. The Tap Room is open from 5 p.m. to 4 a.m., and you don't need to be going to a show to stop in for a beer or two.

L'ACAJOU*

53 West 19th Street (5th/6th Aves)
212-645-1706

A Slice of Northern France in Chelsea

Maybe it's because Danny Kohn's few-frills restaurant is too authentically French; whatever the reason, it doesn't bother him any more that he's never had a major review. He's happy with his steady clientele of locals, and they're happy with him, his food, his wine and, yes, his beer.

Kohn is a quality nut, the kind of host you want making your dinner and selecting your beer. "I carry very few bottled beers because they're just not as good as draft. They're not as fresh," he says. He recently bounced Samuel Adams from his draft list because "they weren't getting it to me fresh enough." L'Acajou, which means "mahogany," offers food with strong Alsatian leanings and a Normandy influence. There are two fixed-price lunch menus, one for under $10 and the other for under $20. The fixed-price supper is under $30 before 8 p.m. Keep your eyes peeled for The Cat.

LAZY BOY SALOON**

154 Mamaroneck Avenue, White Plains
914-761-0272

"Largest Selection of Draught Beer in Westchester"

Since the place opened in April 19○○, co-owner J.R. Cavallaro has built up to 50 beers, more than two dozen of them on draft. The list includes micros that aren't ordinarily seen in these parts, such as New England Atlantic Amber. Other drafts include Catamount Porter, Elm City Ale, Brooklyn Lager, Samuel Adams, Anchor Steam and Rhino Chaser Amber Ale.

The rotating bottle selection is not bad, but should be better when Cavallaro reaches his goal of more micros. The back of the beer menu includes a brewing primer by Terry Soloman, publisher of *Matter World Times*.

Wednesday is micro night, $1 off all pints. There are also beer tasting nights. There's a tastings menu – pick five beers of your own or let the bartender make recommendations – and Cavallaro every now and then opens a few bottles of micros and imports and sets them out on the bar for patrons to sample.

"People who come in here want something different, something special," Cavallaro says. "This isn't a kiddie bar. We get a lot of couples, and people in their late 20s to 40s. The young guys go down the street and drink their Budweiser. This is a friendly place. We've never had a fight in here."

The place has a nice look, newly redone in dark reddish wood with a half wall separating the dining room. There's a pool table in back. The menu is contemporary American, with a good choice of sandwiches, salads, starters, burgers (for under $6) and main courses such as shrimp, pasta and chicken (most under $10 for dinner).

LEFTY LOUIE'S**

1690 York Avenue (89th)
212-988-3947

"A Neighborhood Joint"

Indeed, every neighborhood should have a joint like Lefty Louie's: tasty food, fair prices, good for a drink after work, a family place in the early evening that smoothly shifts into a haven for grownups as night settles on Yorkville.

Owners Michael Hurwitz and Howard Gering cater to the community first and the bar crowd second; thankfully, the community is often found at the bar. And the bar, with eight draft lines and 70-plus bottled beers, is very well stocked.

"We believe in good beer," they say. "We do everything in our power to get people drinking good beer. Doesn't matter if they're four deep at the bar, if somebody asks for a Bud, we tell 'em, 'Look, there are 75 or 80 of the best beers in the world back here, and you want a Bud?' Nine out of 10 times, we can get 'em to try something different, and they like it. Their Budweiser days are done."

Bottled micros include Breckenridge Avalanche and Oatmeal Stout, Brooklyn Brown, Catamount Amber, Celis Pale Bock and White. Bottled imports include various offerings from Samuel Smith's and Lindemans. Draft beer includes Brooklyn Lager, Saranac Pale Ale and Saranac Black and Tan.

Opened in July 1994, Lefty Louie's has been a restaurant or bar or both for at least 100 years, including when this corner of the Upper East Side was run by a local gangster who happened to be a southpaw and whose mother had him christened Louis.

Tucked behind Gracie Mansion, Lefty Louie's current incarnation features a soothing dark red motif, antiques, and a number of big tables that are good for family dining and host a great many kids' birthday parties. The music is easy jazz, and there's a place to park strollers near the entrance. The menu has a list of beers with descriptions, and there's talk of starting some beer tastings.

The menu offers a variety of sandwiches, salads, pastas and meat or fish dishes, nearly all for under $10, which again proves the point that Yorkville isn't really part of the Upper East Side.

LES HALLES*

411 Park Avenue South (28th/29th)
212-679-4111

A Classic French Steakhouse

Don't be put off by the fact that this 40-year-old bistro is a hangout for British and Australian journalists. They're there for the same reasons you are, including the 22-ounce bottles of Fischer, both amber and bitter.

Along with its steaks, chops and sausages in the $15-20 range – on display in the butcher's case at the entrance – co-owner Jose Meirelles keeps Les Halles stocked with Sierra Nevada on draft, bottles of Jenlain and other good brews. A good lunch choice: a big bowl of steamed mussels with fries and one of those large Fischers. For dinner, steak tartare with Sierra. There's also a good menu for wine, port, cognac, armagnac and single malts.

The saying, "Gone to the devil," originated among London lawyers who used to leave that message with their chambers when nipping down to their local, the Devil Tavern.

LIFE CAFE*

343 East 10th Street (Ave B)
212-477-8791

A Bar-Restaurant That Doesn't Need to Imitate Art

The Life presents a distinct attitude, but it's not the sort of attitude one expects in New York. It's friendly, casual, open – much more typical of the Midwest, which happens to be where owner Kathy Kirkpatrick grew up.

"We were kind of a pioneer," she says of her cafe's opening back in the early 1980s, when it was the only restaurant east of First Avenue for several blocks north or south. "Now we're not an outpost, we're a landmark."

Life caters to the neighborhood's – and all of Manhattan's – artsy crowd, whether young and starving or not. The food, a lot of Cal-Mex and vegetarian but also some burgers and seafood, is wholesome, cheap and good, and the beer includes Brooklyn Brown and Saranac Golden Pilsner on draft. A fair number of showbiz types – Woody Harrelson, Iggy Pop, Debra Winger, Matt Dillon (of course) – stop in when they're in town. This is a very good spot for herbal tea, too.

LONDON LENNIE'S**

63-88 Woodhaven Blvd., Queens
718-894-8084

Seafood, See Beer in Rego Park

Founded by a Cockney lad who ran away to sea and settled in Queens in the 1950s, Lennie's is a big family-run restaurant with a horseshoe-shaped bar and a terrific fish and seafood menu. The raw bar – they shuck 'em right there at the bar while customers sip their beer in anticipation – features several varieties of clams and oysters daily.

Other seafood, which Lennie's people hand-pick at 3 a.m. from the Fulton Fish Market, includes stone crabs, tuna, fluke, scrod, scallops, mussels, Dover sole, lobster, triggerfish, sea bass, swordfish, red snapper, tile fish, shark and more. The restaurant is not fancy but appealing, with tables spread out along the big streetfront windows. The wooden dividers separating the booths are topped by translucent panes that provide an art-deco or 1950s feel.

It should be pointed out that the non-seafood offerings can be spectacular, too. At one big New York beer-and-food event, Lennie's chefs stole the show with a fruit cobbler made with hollandaise sauce, cooked in Liefmans Kriek and served with Liefmans Frambozen.

There's a good beer menu, printed with some nice descriptions of styles of beer and particular brands. Harpoon Light, Brooklyn Brown and Heineken are on tap, with a bottle selection including Paulaner Pilsner and Hefe-Weizen, Hoegaarden, Duvel, Pike Place, Young's Special London Ale, Bateman's XXXB, Affligem Tripel and Samuel Smith's Oatmeal Stout. David Kaiser, the manager who has done so much to bring in new beers, is also considering doing some beer and seafood dinners.

Even for diehard Manhattanites who typically spend more time in Europe than in the outer boroughs, this is a place that makes it worth getting out the map and the passport. Call the people at London Lennie's, tell them where you are, and they'll tell you the best way to get to them – and their beer and oysters.

"When I realized that what I had turned out to be was a lousy, two-bit pool hustler and drunk, I wasn't depressed at all. I was glad to have a profession."
Danny McGoorty

LONG ISLAND BREWING CO.

111 Jericho Turnpike, Jericho
516-334-BREW

A Brewpub for the Masses

The biggest complaint about LIBC, as it's known locally, is that it's too crowded, especially on weekends. When it's busy, even on some week nights, there's valet parking only. LIBC opened in December 1994 and became an immediate hit, drawing people from a broad stretch of Long Island and the city.

It's an impressive use of space, with the brewery up front, in between the big window and the copper-topped bar, which makes any stool a good vantage point for watching the brewers climb around on the catwalks. The main bar area is decorated with some post-modern murals, while the sunken dining room, including a little mezzanine, is jammed with interesting beerphernalia. The food is good, plentiful and reasonably priced. Upstairs there's a coffee bar and bar featuring live music and comedy, and a different perspective on the brewing works.

As with virtually every new brewpub, LIBC draws complaints from area home brewers, who all think they could do better than brewmaster Mark Burford if they had the chance. Burford, himself the owner of a homebrew supply store, is a patient kind of guy, however, and really tries to take time to talk to fellow brewers and show them around. He gives tours by appointment and every Sunday from 11:30 to 2:30 during the Brewmaster's Brunch, a hearty buffet.

Perhaps the most generous gesture to home brewers, and certainly the bravest, is Burford's "volunteer" program under which he lets home brewers come in and work with him on Mondays, Tuesdays and Wednesdays. It's a rare opportunity for home brewers who are curious about what it's like to step up a few notches.

Burford's beers include a Lager, a Porter, an Ale, an Octoberfest, a Stout, a Steam, a Scotch Ale and various fruit beers including a Raspberry Wheat, a Cranberry Ale, a Blueberry Ale and a Pumpkin Ale. He also serves a cask-conditioned ale pulled through an 1885 beer engine that he's reconditioned.

LOX AROUND THE CLOCK*

676 Sixth Avenue (21st)
212-691-3535

Jivin' Jewish

Lox Around the Clock is all things to all people, or seemingly at least all Chelsea residents, from the old Jewish folks to the young hip-hoppers, as long as they're not looking for uptown decor or uptown prices. It's furnished, if that's the right word, with old metal chairs, some of them painted yellow, and a variety of tables that appear to have been discarded from luncheonettes and private kitchens circa 1953. The lights are hung haphazardly and the music is good new rock or old rhythm 'n' blues. The menu is a similar jumble of traditional Jewish cooking and regulation deli sandwiches, salads, soups, burgers and pasta. Lots of people bring in kids during the day.

The beer list is fluid, in every sense of the word, with Saranac Black and Tan, Bass and Leinenkugel Red on draft. A few other micros, including Sierra Nevada and New England, appear at least semi-regularly in bottles or on tap at the good-sized wooden bar where a surprising number of people stop in just for a beer.

Jeff Baskin, the bar manager who built the beer list, is a good guy who's happy to talk with customers and has a remarkable memory for faces and beer orders. Odds are he'll remember you and what you were drinking last time you were in, even if it's been months.

LUDLOW STREET CAFE*

165 Ludlow Street (Houston/Stanton)
212-353-0536

Hot Music, Hot Food, Cold Beer

The live music seven nights a week is what
draws people to this Cajun restaurant: country
one night, blues the next, rock the night after
that. The restaurant and bar are open at 6 p.m.,
but the music doesn't begin until around 11 p.m.
(and lasts til the 4 a.m. closing) in what is com-
monly regarded as one of the best live music
rooms in New York. No less than *Rolling Stone*
called it "the hippest place" in Manhattan as
recently as 1994.

The cafe holds fewer than 100, including dining tables, booths and stools lined along the
Formica bar, and there are only two draft lines,
but they pour Sierra Nevada Pale Ale (or Porter)
and Dortmunder Dark. The bottle selection
includes Saranac, any variety of which is good
beer, and Dixie Blackened Voodoo, which is
notable more for its rarity north of the Mason-
Dixon line than for its quality.

McFEELEY'S*

847 Union Street (6th/7th Aves), Brooklyn
718-638-0099

A Park Slope Bistro

Families are common early in the evening and
on weekends, with a good mix of dining and
drinking later. The bar features Saranac Gold,
Anchor Steam, Brooklyn and Sierra Nevada on
draft, while the dining room has an upscale
menu including leg of lamb stew, baked red
snapper and other main courses in the $12-16
range. This is a reliable neighborhood place,
with a nice dark-wood look.

McSORLEY'S OLD ALE HOUSE

15 E. 7th Street (2nd/3rd Aves)
212-473-9148

A Landmark Since 1854

Arguably the most famous bar in New York, McSorley's literally has the history of the city on its walls, including photographs by Brady and many others, historic documents and just plain American arcania. Abe Lincoln reputedly dropped by after a speech at Cooper Union, and the current owner, Matthew Maher, has an autograph to prove it. Somewhere.

Maher, a professional Irish character often found sitting on an empty keg outside the front door, has owned the bar since the 1970s, when it briefly became a national story after women protested its long men-only rule. Since then, Maher has bowed to the times to the extent that he's even had a women's restroom installed. But other traditions at McSorley's persist, including the rule that the beer, served in nine-ounce steins that can be one-third foam, must be ordered two at a time.

Good beer drinkers might think that's unfair because they may not want to drink a second one after the first. McSorley's serves only its own dark and light "ales," which are actually made by large and not particularly distinguished commercial breweries. In truth, however, McSorley's draws few quality beer drinkers just for the beer, or for its modest but reliable pub grub.

The place is worth a stop – if the line outside isn't too long – just to soak up a little history. For soaking up good beer, walk a short way down East 7th Street to Burp Castle or Brewsky's, two of the finest beer bars anywhere.

MAIN STREET*

446 Columbus Avenue (81st)
212-873-5025

Family Style, a la Upper West Side

Main Street is a typical piece of Columbus Avenue geography, meaning it can trace its pedigree of trendiness back to the Roaring Eighties, when it was home to movie director Dino DeLaurentis' spectacular but ill-fated DDL Foodshow. The current version serves American food American style, with big tables where big groups can share big portions from big platters.

A feature is all-you-can-eat mashed potatoes on a menu that includes "sharing" starters such as Cajun popcorn for $16 and barbecued chicken kabobs with fresh fruit chutney for $11. Main dishes, which serve 2-3, include wild Tchoupitoulas gumbo, roast turkey dinner, crab cakes and leg of lamb, all for $23 and up. Desserts are homemade pies, chocolate cake, Heathbar crunch cake, puddings, splits and sundaes.

The brick walls, columns and arches are central to the restaurant's solid look, and the good-sized bar at the entrance, with a couple dozen stools, has Pete's on draft and Sierra Nevada, Telluride, Pete's and Dock Street in bottles. The manager, Steve Sher, looks kind of like Kevin Costner, and plays the Talking Heads nice and loud on the good sound system.

In Victorian times, British soldiers serving in India, the "jewel in the crown" of the British empire, complained about beer arriving stale from the homeland. Knowing that hops act as a preservative, English brewers developed the heavily-hopped India Pale Ale to survive the long voyage around the Cape of Good Hope.

MANCHESTER**

920 Second Avenue (48th/49th)
212-223-7484

"Life's Too Short To Drink Cheap Beer"

That's Manchester's motto. It's not original, but there are unlikely to be any objections among the beer drinkers who have been living by that credo for years. Like they teach you in journalism school, you can't copyright a fact.

This is a good honest bar on the eastern side of Midtown, with room for 50 people "and 90 if the Knicks are in the playoffs," according to Caroline Torres, a manager. There's a respectable menu of bar food, including ribs, shepherd's pie, fish ' n' chips, and finger food such as wings, skins, nachos and a ploughman's tray of cheese, Branston pickle, pickled onions, bread, butter and (unheard of in a pub in England) apple sauce.

With its five TVs, Manchester likes to characterize itself as a "modern British sports bar," which sounds in theory like the worst of both worlds. But don't be put off; as the Bard should have said, the beer's the thing. Manchester has 18 on draft, including Sierra Nevada and Fullers ESB, and more than 40 in bottles, including:

From England, Old Peculier, Thomas Hardy's Ale and Bateman's Victory Ale; from Germany, Paulaner Hefe-Weizen, Salvator and Oktoberfest; from Belgium, Duvel, Lindemans Peche and Framboise, Chimay Grand Reserve, Corsendonk Brown and Dentergems.

The American microbrews include Anchor Steam, Brooklyn Brown Ale, Black Dog Ale, Black Voodoo and Catamount Amber.

Manchester, which is also diligent about getting in special and seasonal brews, draws a mostly white-collar crowd after work, and late at night is dominated by mostly young guys watching sports. "A lot of women come in here, including by themselves, but this is not a pickup bar,"

Torres says. The 4-7 p.m. Happy Hour is usually packed, with $4.50 pints marked down to $3.25.

The bar's look is a mix of brick-wall trendy and black-and-white diner. Torres says Manchester's staff tries to be personal; someone coming in alone is often included in conversations with bartenders and regulars. She also says that while the staff is happy to talk about the beer, "Our customers know beer. They're intelligent. We're not trying to educate anybody."

MANHATTAN BREWING CO.

40-42 Thompson Street (Broome)
212-925-1515

Is It Open?

That's the question. Call before you make the trip to see if Manhattan Brewing, the city's first brewpub back in the mid 1980s, is back in business. Beset by financial problems in recent years, Manhattan Brewing has closed and reopened and closed again amid a difficult restructuring effort.

The biggest blow came in 1994 when the brewery could no longer afford the services of brewmaster Garrett Oliver; Manhattan's loss was Brooklyn's gain. Meanwhile, there's little point at this writing of going into any detail about Manhattan's beer or food or anything else. In whatever form it re-opens – and here's hoping it does – it will be like starting over.

Thomas Hardy was a friend of the grandfather of Christopher Pope, current head of the Eldridge Pope brewery in Dorset.

MANHATTAN CHILI CO.**

1500 Broadway (43rd Street)
212-734-8666

Chili, Children, Cheap & Cheerful

Anyone who has ever taken kids into the Times Square area knows the combination of excitement and trepidation that Manhattan offers. Yes, you can see a great play, but you may also have to drag the kids past peep shows. Daddy, why are those men dressed like women? Why don't those ladies on the posters have any clothes on? Mommy, where is there a place to pee? Kids, where can dad and mom get a beer?

Manhattan Chili, along with neighboring Virgil's Real Barbecue, is an oasis in the Times Square area offering the rare combination of cheap, cheerful, good food and good beer. Variations of chili are the specialty, naturally, but there are also soups, burgers, salads and other Mexican dishes. It's possible to get a bowl of good chili and wash it down with good beer for $10. And there's a kids' menu for under $5.

Bruce and Luba Sterman, the owners, took a big chance when they closed their chili restaurant in Greenwich Village and moved to Times Square. They took another chance when they decided to concentrate on one brewery – Catamount. Both risks have paid off. Manhattan Chili offers Catamount Amber, Porter, Gold and seasonals such as Bock, American Wheat, Octoberfest and Christmas Ale.

Catamount was an inspiration born of perspiration; Bruce Sterman talked to and visited many micros, and decided to limit his beer menu to a single brewery (plus New England Light) in order to guarantee freshness. "I really wanted to make a quality statement," he says.

Sterman recounts with relish how one macro brewery after another came in when he opened and asked how many cases he wanted of Bud,

Miller, Coors. "You guys don't get it," he explained as he threw them out.

Just as chili attracts a cross-section of humanity, Sterman has found that people can be converted to quality beer if they just try a good microbrew. His crowd includes not only relieved parents who have found a place to eat and have a beer, and relieved kids who have found a place to pee, but also a healthy mix of Broadway "kids," the singers, dancers and bit players, and stagehands and technical people who make the shows run behind the scenes.

One final tip: anyone who nails down a place on a stool in the window by 9:30 on New Year's Eve can drink Catamount in relative warmth and comfort with a good view of the revelers thronging to Times Square and, ultimately, the big ball dropping at midnight.

MORAN'S*

145 Tenth Avenue (19th)
212-989-5689

Lace-Curtain Irish and Elegant Seafood

Moran's may be the only restaurant in Manhattan with five working fireplaces. In a town where the classification "Irish" conjures up noisy bars serving pub grub, this is a genteel family-run and family-oriented Chelsea establishment that combines comforting and comfortable surroundings with good seafood.

Most main courses are around or under $20. Seafood pasta is a favorite, and so are salmon Wellington, Connemara stuffed sole and bouillabaise. Moran's surf and turf is filet mignon and a seven-ounce lobster tail.

The kitchen-bar area, with old cash registers, copper kettles and fittings and one of the best old tin ceilings in town, leads into several dining rooms with a variety of tables small and large that suit eating with kids or, in quieter corners, *a deux*. It's not unusual to see adults lingering at their table while the kids – who are welcome to wander as long as they're not running and shouting – gather wide-eyed around the lobster tank or check out the rest of the place, including the sparkling crystal displays.

There are six draft lines offering Brooklyn Lager, Pete's Wicked Ale, Samuel Adams, Guinness, Harp and Bass.

MUGS ALEHOUSE***

125 Bedford Avenue (N. 10th), Brooklyn
718-384-8494

A Beer Outpost in the Artists Colony

This is a serious beer bar in the middle of one of the most interesting areas of New York City – Williamsburg, home to Polish, Italian and other ethnic groceries, a handful of quietly good bar-restaurants such as nearby Teddy's, some enterprising new businesses, some old-time warehouse and distribution operations, and a great many working painters, sculptors and other artists.

Williamsburg, only one stop out of Manhattan on the L subway line, may one day go the route of SoHo, which was much like this area 30 years ago. But for now it shows no sign of surrendering its rough charm to gentrification. Make no mistake, despite the appeal of busier streets like Bedford and Berry, this is not a neighborhood for leaving your car with Christmas presents on the seat or wandering off on dark side streets alone at night.

But you'd need a good reason to wander away from Mugs Alehouse. The building looks like it was once one of those no-nonsense gin mills, but today the place is refurbished and clean, dominated by brass and wood. The owners, Ed and Halina Berestecki, are a really nice couple, and you'll be friends for life if you ask about the baby.

There are 24 draft lines and 70-plus bottled beers. The drafts include Catamount Amber,

Paulaner Salvator, Rogue-N-Berry, Rogue Dry-Hopped Red, Saranac Golden Pilsner, Young's Oatmeal Stout and Sierra Nevada Porter. Also Brooklyn Lager, which rolls out the barrels from the Brooklyn Brewery warehouse just around the corner. Ask at Mugs if Brooklyn has opened its new brewery and tasting room; if so, tear yourself away from Mugs, at least briefly, to sample Brooklyn brewmaster Garrett Oliver's latest at the ale-only brewery he's designed from scratch in an old bakery.

Mugs' bottled beer includes Chimay Grand Reserve, Lindemans Framboise, St. Sixtus Abbey and many others, including a growing selection of vintage beers from Thomas Hardy's ('86, '89), several Lambics, and others. The crowd is generally 25-50, a mixture of artists, neighborhood workers, and a few young professionals who work in Manhattan but live locally for the great space and cheap prices. The bar encourages women and couples, and the two unobtrusive TV sets, when they're on, are as likely to be playing "Banacek" or "Brady Bunch" reruns as sports.

There are always seasonal beers, and a different micro or import is featured each month in a $2 pint special.

The Swiss beer Hexenbrau means "witch's brew," and is especially good after dinner, for casting a spell on fruit desserts.

NACHO MAMA'S BURRITOS**

2867 Broadway (111th/112th)
212-666-6187

Mexican, Micros and Motherhood

Don't ask co-owner Joshua Mandel about micro-brewed beer or his own Mexican food, and especially about the two together, unless you're ready for a nonstop rapid-fire New Yawk mono-logue. He's good value, and so is his place. On their takeout menu, he and partner Larry Good enunciate their philosophy "to be fair, honest and verbose." Nacho Mama's gets high praise from the Tex-Mex crowd for serving its burritos with the guacamole and sour cream on the side, so you can do your own blend and practice some sogginess control. There are also tacos, enchiladas, salads and a variety of appetizers.

Nacho Mama's gets high marks from the beer crowd for its devotion to micros. "I gottatellya," says Mandel, himself a home brewer. "Beer is the most incredible thing that's ever come my way. I mean, food is great but beer, beer is incredible. We can tell which beers I'm drinking around here by which ones we're re-ordering the most." The 20 bottle beers are all domestic, nearly all micros, and Mandel is expanding the list as students and other customers in the Columbia University area become more adventuresome.

"We're the beer focus for this neighborhood," Mandel says. "Because of us, the deli's and the other restaurants around here are getting micros in. We're creating the demand."

Nacho Mama's is a second-story job, up a narrow staircase to an irregularly shaped room that can be safely described as without frills. Lunches and evenings are busy, and the tiny bar area is likely to become even busier when Mandel puts in the six draft lines he's been talking about. Among other things, Nacho Mama's scores a triple bullseye on that philosophy.

NORTH STAR PUB***

93 South Street (Fulton)
212-509-6757

Olde England By The Sea(port)

The North Star is many New Yorkers' nominee for the most authentic – and best – English-style pub in Manhattan. There really is a lot to admire about this pub, owned by a Welsh architect who has brought in a drinks list that in fact leaves most British pubs in the shade.

The eight draft lines, with servings in 20-ounce imperial pints or 10-ounce half-pints, deliver seasonals such as Young's Winter Warmer and Fuller's ESB, along with more familiar standards such as Fuller's London Pride and McEwans Export. The 14 bottled beers include St. Andrews Ale, Royal Oak Ale, Bateman's XXXB, Thomas Hardy's Ale and a winning quartet from Tadcaster: Samuel Smith's Nut Brown Ale, Pale Ale, Taddy Porter and (in season) Winter Welcome.

Located right across the street from the entrance to the South Street Seaport museum and shopping complex, the North Star's pub grub is properly seafood-leaning. The following are served with the authentic English mushy peas: fish sandwich, ale-battered scallops, fish 'n' chips, scallops 'n' chips, shrimp 'n' chips, and chips 'n' chips, along with classics such as shepherd's pie, bangers and mash, sausage 'n' beans 'n' chips, ploughman's and, for dessert, bread 'n' single malt whisky pudding. There is a fine range of single malts, by the way, with three options for tasting flights.

Deven Black, the manager, is a personable guy, a journalist gone straight – or, at least, sort of – who knows his beers aren't to everyone's taste. He laughs at the people who come in and balk at trying a dark beer. "They say they don't like the color," he says. "I say, hey, try it first. Judging by color was supposed to have gone out in the '60s."

"If we can't convince you to try something, we'll send you somewhere else, but the tasting is free," he says. "For people who aren't sure about ale – many women, for example – we start them on Newcastle Brown, which is a little sweet."

If a beer doesn't move, however, it's gone. "There's a big emphasis on keeping the beer fresh," Black says. "The beers we have, we sell 'em fast. Kegs are rarely on more than 24 hours. And we clean out the entire system every two weeks."

The North Star's bartenders are all either British, Irish or Americans who have lived or traveled extensively in Britain and Ireland. There is a low turnover: only one new bartender in the last six years. Say hello to Stuffy if he's pulling pints.

The tables outside in summer are great for watching the crowds thronging in and out of the Seaport, or for sitting and reading. The North Star, like many pubs in England, has a distinct affection for the written word, as evidenced in the small library of beer and whisky books that patrons are welcome to browse.

Every couple of months, the pub also publishes what may be the best tavern newsletter around, *North Star Pub Notes*. Ranging from informative to hilarious, the newsletter provides information on events both serious (charity drives) and frivolous (party for St. George's Day, right after the religious service). There's news about new beers or whiskies – the North Star recently scored a rare bottle of Bowmore Black, and offers tastes at $30 for a 1.75-ounce serving – and a calendar of what happened on that date in history ("British colonists first taste popcorn, 1630. Say they wish they had something to watch…") and Top Ten (or 9, or 11) lists. Signs you are a beer geek: No. 3, That really is a church key in your pocket…No. 2, You think a plain white T-shirt is a misprint…No. 1, You thought registering for the draft was a keg party."

NOSMO KING**

54 Varick Street (S. of Canal)
212-966-1239

Healthy Food and Beer

Odd. An odd location, an odd menu (healthy, vegetarian), an odd name, an odd but comfortable decor. For the many who don't mind the odd, or occasionally seek it out, that's fine. There's certainly nothing odd about the beer list, or the special six-course beer and food tasting menu at Nosmo King.

There aren't many draft lines, but they are likely to serve up Brooklyn Brown, Catamount, Dock Street Bohemian, Harpoon or one of several rotating seasonals. The roster of bottles includes Boont Amber, Castelain Jade, Geary's Ale, Grant's Scottish and Weiss, Harpoon Lager and Light, Lindemans Peche, New York Harbor Dark, Paulaner, Pinkus and Rodenbach.

Odd or not, owner Steve Frankel and chef Alan Harding have made this is a very good restaurant that stresses organic and non-dairy and non-meat ingredients, and makes an effort to match the natural foods with craft-brewed beer. The staffers are knowledgeable about beer, and the place may be holding some beer dinners in the future.

Nosmo King has a good-sized bar, and diners downstairs can sit in big padded booths beneath some extravagant old chandeliers. There's also a mezzanine above. About the odd name, if you didn't get it by now: No Smoking. Nosmo King.

NO-TELL MOTEL*

167 Avenue A (10th)
212-533-0709

Cheap Sex in the East Village

In the era of bars with themes, why not a place that celebrates illicit sex? Decorated with oversized playing cards of scantily-clad pinups, the No-Tell Motel celebrates the cheap one-night stand in the spirit of the roadside joint that rents rooms by the hour. The place doesn't open until 8 or 8:30 most evenings, and doesn't get busy until later, when at times it can become an aggressive pickup joint. There's not a vast selection of bottled beer and there are only three draft lines, but those typically carry quality brews such as Saranac and Brooklyn Lager.

OCEANA**

55 East 54th Street (Madison/Park)
212-759-5941

Moonen Over Manhattan

If only there were more chefs like Rick Moonen, formerly of the Water Club. Along with Paul McLaughlin, the general manager, Moonen has made Oceana one of the brightest dining spots in Midtown, a true balance of quality and service for the 1990s and beyond.

While the restaurant's food, mostly from the sea, has been extremely well reviewed since it opened in early 1992, Moonen continually has looked for ways to improve. One of the biggest improvements has been in the beer menu, which was expanded to include Duvel, Chimay Blue, Lindemans Framboise and others. "The beer market has really changed," McLaughlin says. "In the last few years we've found it necessary to go to better quality beer, just as we've gone to better quality food."

Oceana is not cheap; prices start at close to $30 for three-course fixed-price dinners featuring starters such as lobster ravioli or rock shrimp and scallop cakes, and entrees such as pan-seared skate wing, and grilled swordfish, snapper and salmon. The crowd in the cool, pastel dining room is mostly corporate at lunch, and a mix of corporate types, tourists and well-off couples about town in the evening.

O'DONOHUE'S TAVERN*

66 Main Street, Nyack
914-358-0180

A Rivertown Tavern

Anyone who grew up in a river town will feel instantly at home in this old, down-at-the-heels joint with its pews by the front door, handful of tables in back, fake brick floor, Formica bartop and old guys nursing taps at the bar. Barry Koch, who says his boss of 13 years, Kevin O'Donohue, provides the place with its offbeat personality, declares that this is the only bar in the neighborhood that hasn't been "redesigned, if you know what I mean" to look more upscale.

Koch says the clientele "ranges from blue collar to literati – a lot of writers; Carson McCullers was a regular here – with very little yuppie in between." This is the sort of place where Jonathan Demme, the movie director, would hang out – and does. The 10 draft beers include Harpoon IPA, Brooklyn Brown, Samuel Adams, Sierra Nevada and Pete's. The bottles include Samuel Smith's Nut Brown Ale. Food includes pot pies, chili and sandwiches under $7.

"Only Irish coffee provides in a single glass all four essential food groups: alcohol, caffeine, sugar and fat."
Alex Levine

OLD TOWN BAR*

45 East 18th Street (Park/Broadway)
212-529-6732

Aptly Named, a Step Back a Century

This is a beautiful old chunk of Gramercy Park history, and many of the furnishings appear to be original from the saloon's 1892 opening. The long bar's brass railing, the sturdy polished-wood booths and the large glazed mirrors help evoke the Gay Nineties.

There's a standard menu, but the burgers are regarded as among the best served by any bar in Manhattan. Among those who favor wings, this place also gets a star. But the Old Town is less a restaurant than another venerable saloon down the street, Pete's Tavern. Unfortunately, like Pete's, its beer choices could be broader. There are eight taps, and the drafts include Brooklyn, Sierra Nevada and Murphy's Stout. There's also Genny Cream, for those who grew up on the stuff and want a walk down nostalgia lane – and a reminder of why they left it behind.

THE OYSTER BAR

Grand Central Station (Downstairs)
212-490-6650

Manhattan on a Half Shell

Whether or not this is the best-known restaurant in Manhattan, it's arguably the most romantic: not just for the emphasis on oysters, a renowned aphrodisiac, but also for the way the Oyster Bar epitomizes so much of New York. It's big, busy, anonymous, can be cheap or expensive, can be a lifetime habit or a once-in-a-lifetime experience, and attracts people who are on the move, figuratively or literally.

The Oyster Bar has a lot of mediocre beer and some good beer, notably Brooklyn Lager on draft and a few others in bottles. Try Samuel

Smith's Oatmeal Stout with a dozen oysters, especially if you're visiting from somewhere that doesn't have a lot of stout or fresh oysters. It's part of the romance of the greatest city on earth.

PARKS' PLACE**

121 Mineola Boulevard, Mineola
516-248-2686

A Mineola Monopoly on Micros

It's too bad, but Hasbro, the toy company, has forced John Parks, the owner of Parks' Place, to get rid of all the Monopoly theme stuff, including the signs, that decorated the place after he opened it in 1993.

But that's okay – his new theme is good beer, and lots of it. Parks was a committed, confirmed vodka drinker until St. Patrick's Day 1994. That night, when the restaurant slowed down, his sons, both in their early twenties, persuaded their dad to come out with them and try some of that new microbrewed beer. "I tried a few of them and they were good," Parks Senior recalls. "Then I tried Brooklyn Brown and fell in love with it. Now I think beer is the wave of the future."

Parks is up to 31 draft lines, with a selection that includes Bass, Guinness, Pete's, Pilsner Urquell, Woodpecker, Amberley, Catamount Porter, Saranac Pale Ale, Samuel Adams, Dinkel Acker, Apple Jack, Harpoon Light, Young's Oatmeal Stout and, of course, Brooklyn Brown.

With its lace-curtained dining room off the tap room, Parks' Place has an Irish feel and an all-American menu that ranges from Chinatown pork dumplings to roast beef to vegetarian pizza, all at extremely reasonable prices. There is also a kids' menu offering a burger, pasta, cheese pizza or tuna melt.

PARK SLOPE BREWERY

356 6th Avenue (5th), Brooklyn
718-788-1756

A Craftsman's Dream Come True

Just from looking around the Park Slope brewpub, it's obvious that Steve Deptula, who did all his own work, is a heckuva carpenter. From drinking his beer, it's also obvious that he's a heckuva brewer.

Park Slope has been widely acclaimed as perhaps the best of the brewpub-restaurants in New York City in the mid-1990s. And while its ranking is sure to be challenged by other new places that seem to be opening every few months, Deptula doesn't need to worry about his regulars defecting – as long, of course, as he keeps crafting good beer.

Deptula, a longtime cabinetmaker who began home brewing in 1990, is making 10 beers on rotation in the basement brewery he literally welded together for a mere $45,000. He's proud of his setup, and rightly so; if he's around, and he usually is, having a pint or four himself, ask for a tour of the premises.

Deptula, whose brother-in-law financed the new business and was rewarded with a usually-crowded brewpub that began making a profit soon after it opened in August 1994, has had particular success with his California Pale Ale, Porter and Pumpkin Ale. Still a homebrewer at heart, he often hosts meetings of local homebrewers down in the brewery, sampling their stuff and then giving them an advance tasting of his newest Barleywine or other brew.

Deptula admits to tweaking the recipes for a time after Jack Streich, the well-known brewpub startup consultant, showed him how to brew in commercial batches, and he confesses to occasional mistakes such as the one time he "rushed" a beer and it ended up flat. "Never again," he says. "I learned my lesson. But now I think we're where we want to be in terms of the beer. Even

Garrett Oliver, the Brooklyn Brewery brewmaster, has been saying nice things about us."

And why not? Park Slope is a good place, full of families during the day – "It kind of surprised me...I had to go out and buy a bunch of high chairs the first week," Deptula says – and a mix of couples, singles and groups during the evenings. The food menu is modest, with rings, nachos, wings, five salads, six sandwiches (including a veggie burger) and five entrees including chili, macaroni and cheese, kielbasa and sauerkraut, fish and chips, and rosemary polenta. There's also a kids menu and drinks such as egg creams and birch beer on tap.

None of the food costs anywhere near the most expensive thing on the menu – a pitcher of the beer of your choice for $13.

PECULIER PUB***

145 Bleecker Street (Thompson)
212-353-1327

Home on the Strange

The Peculier Pub isn't really all that peculiar, except for the fact that it has 370 beers, at last estimate. That is no misprint: 370 beers, the widest selection in New York. If you're eager for an Edelhell or scorched for a Scaldis or salivating for a St. Amand or hot for a Hexenbrau or dying for a Dock Street (all of which you could or should be), the Peculier Pub's the place.

The beer list runs to six columns of small type spread over two full-size pages. The 11 draft lines change often, but typically include a mix of micros, imports, seasonals and, too bad, a couple of drab mass-produced domestics. There are close to 100 microbrews in bottles, not counting the ones with national marketing campaigns that aren't really micros any more. Last winter there were 15 seasonals at the Peculier Pub.

From Rogue alone, there's the Red, the Ale, the Shakespeare Stout and the Berry. Breckenridge supplies Oatmeal Stout, IPA, Avalanche and Mountain Wheat. From the American godfather of hops, Bert Grant, there's Grant's Celtic Ale, Scottish Ale, Imperial Stout, IPA, Weiss and Spiced Ale.

Let's just say there's no need to buy a newspaper to bring to the Peculier Pub, even if you're alone. Tommy Chow, the owner who enjoys his reputation as one of the beer pioneers – and one of the real characters – of New York bar circles, makes sure the beer menu provides plenty of good reading.

The Peculier Pub, with a capacity of about 180 under its original tin ceiling, has the feel of an old downstairs college bar, with big, plain wooden tables and booths that can accommodate a crowd of pitcher-drinkers. The walls are decorated with beer mats and Linda Kennedy, a manager, makes no bones about this being a bar "for beer heads." Kennedy, who along with other bartenders has to pass Chow's "beer tests" about what's on the Peculier Pub's beer list, how the beers taste and even how they're brewed, says the beer aficionados mostly come in during the week. On weekends, the place turns into more of what it looks like – a college bar, with a mixture of tourists and the Bridge and Tunnel Crowd in from New Jersey, Long Island, upstate New York and Connecticut.

Here are Kennedy's words of wisdom for patrons: "We don't take credit cards. No cigar smoking. The staff has been described as vengeful and moody, and that's about right. We're New Yorkers. But we prefer to think of ourselves as knowledgeable and efficient. We're not chatty, unless you want to talk about beer."

There's a 15 percent gratuity automatically included in your tab.

"There is nothing for a case of nerves like a case of beer."
                                           Joan Goldstein

PETE'S TAVERN

129 East 18th Street (Irving)
212-473-7676

Back in Time in Gramercy Park

Pete's Tavern was established in 1864, and 40
years later was a hangout of the writer O. Henry,
whose short stories about life in the big city
made him the equivalent of a rock star – or at
least Steven Spielberg – in New York at the turn
of the century. Look for the booth where Henry
is reputed to have written perhaps his most
famous story, "The Gift of the Magi." This is an
old-fashioned corner saloon, with Sinatra on the
juke and corned beef, pastrami and roast beef on
the wheat or rye. The long bar has Sierra
Nevada on tap, but a place like this deserves and
demands a better selection of beer.

PICHOLINE*

35 West 64th Street (Broadway)
212-724-8585

Lincoln Center Elegance

Along with nearby Iridium, this is a great place
to go before or after the opera, theater, ballet or
symphony. Picholine offers elegance without
being ostentatious. The long narrow room, with
its subdued lighting, is just the sort of place to
have a meal for an occasion to match one of
those special evenings at Lincoln Center. Chef
Terrence Brennan's menu, featuring seafood but
also offering chicken and steak, lists entrees
averaging about $25. The wine list is expansive
and expensive, while the beer includes several
good micros and imports. Unlike some of the
better restaurants moving toward gourmet beer,
Picholine's small bar welcomes drinkers who are
just stopping in for one or two on their way somewhere else. But it's not a place to wear jeans.

PRINCE STREET BAR & RESTAURANT*

125 Prince Street (Wooster)
212-228-8130

A Kid-Friendly Soho Bistro

Light and airy, this restaurant is popular among Soho workers and shoppers, particularly those with little kids who know how unusual it is to find a place that allows strollers inside. The Prince Street Bar has a place to park strollers, and has booster seats for toddlers. But the managers hasten to point out this is not just a family place. "We get a lot of young models in here, too," one of them says.

The food features good portions at fair prices, with an emphasis on burgers and Indonesian along with the usual pasta and salad variations. Only a few dishes on the four-page menu cost more than $10.

Chris Polsinetti, the assistant manager, is a home brewer, but so far he's only been able to get Brooklyn Brown, Samuel Adams, Bass and a daily special on draft. The bottle selection is undistinguished. Let's hope he keeps steadily building up the list.

French *bière de gardes* are made with ale yeast, but cold stored, like a lager. They typically have a long, winey finish.

PUGSLEY'S PUB***

Washington & Albany Streets
212-385-4900

The Small But Perfectly Formed
Downtown "Micro Pub"

The two guys wearing dusty work clothes bellied up to the bar next to the two guys wearing distinctly non-dusty business suits. "I didn't expect to find a bar like this around here," one of the construction workers told the other. "Me neither," his buddy replied. "But my mom would be proud of me. She always hoped I would make it to Wall Street."

In a city known for rewarding those who seek out its nooks and crannies, this tiny bar is one of the best surprises lower Manhattan can offer the quality-beer drinker. Only 600 square feet and with just a handful of stools at the bar and in front of the windows, Pugsley's nonetheless is a Financial District magnet for those of us who prefer unpretentious neighborhood taverns. The 10 draft lines typically offer Sierra Nevada Pale Ale, Harpoon Ale, Brooklyn Brown, Brooklyn Lager, Saranac Golden Pilsner, Dock Street Bohemian Pilsner, Harpoon Light and a seasonal or two. A pint, as of spring 1995, was only $3.50, served in a solid mug. A liter was $6. A variety of seasonals, both in bottles and on draft, are always available. "We do beer, wine and shots. No mixed drinks," Julie and Sandra, the personable blonde bartenders, tell befuddled martini drinkers who stumble in from the nearby World Trade Center.

Pugsley's is a rare but happy meeting of big business and craft brewing. Jeffrey Jacobs, then the food and drinks manager at the vast Marriott hotel and conference center (50 West Street), couldn't figure out what to do with the small corner of retail-zoned space around at the back, at the corner of Albany and Washington. He sought advice from Steve Hindy, the president of the Brooklyn Brewery, who suggested a brewpub.

Hindy brought in Alan Pugsley, the English chemist who has helped with startups for three dozen micros and brewpubs on this side of the pond. Pugsley found the space inappropriate for a brewpub but Jacobs decided to launch what the Marriott now calls "a micro pub exclusively serving micro-brewed beers...beers made the old-fashioned way, with care and love in smaller quantities and with the finest ingredients." Jacobs, now manager of the Brasserie in Midtown, put Pugsley's name on the pub, and incorporated some of Pugsley's brewing trademarks, including a brick-lined, circular "brewhouse" that actually encloses the restrooms.

Pugsley's remains part of the Marriott complex, but is remarkably independent, with no obvious links to the hotel. The bartenders don't wear Marriott duds, for example, and hotel guests have to go outside and walk around the corner just like the rest of us.

The biggest drawback to Pugsley's is that it remains tied to commuters' hours. It is typically open from noon to 10 p.m. on weekdays, and not at all on Saturday or Sunday. That's right: this bar is closed on weekends.

Another point: unlike some other beer bars, Pugsley's is not a male-dominated place. It's not at all unusual to see as many women as men, both groups of women and women coming in by themselves, at the bar.

Pugsley's grub, at reasonable prices, includes chili, burgers, mustard pretzels, onion rings, Cajun fries, sandwiches, wings, and fried chicken, but most drinkers manage to subsist on peanuts in two big barrels, one of them hot and spicy. Free copies of *Ale Street News* are usually stacked by the door.

All in all, this bar is a great find for all good beer drinkers, even those whose moms wouldn't be so proud to find them on Wall Street.

RIVERRUN**

176 Franklin Street (Hudson/Greenwich)
212-966-3894

"The Tribeca Pioneer"

Famous on several levels, riverrun is perhaps known foremost as the first good restaurant in the rise of Tribeca on the New York trendiness scale. Though it has lost some of its luster to the nearby TriBeCa Grill, partly owned by Robert DeNiro, local lore holds that DeNiro himself is just as likely to be spotted at a quiet table near the back of riverrun.

The restaurant is also famous for its menu and its good new-American food. A few samples: blackened chicken on rye sandwich, chicken and apple omelet, Mom's meatloaf, steamed mussels, chicken pot pie, stir-fried fettucine and vegetables in garlic and olive oil. Indeed, many of the dishes on riverrun's menu have become standard at newer American restaurants throughout the city.

The beer list has been as much a pioneer as the location and the food. riverrun was one of the first good restaurants to make an effort with the beer list, and owner Don Berger is not about to take his beer for granted now. There's a five-beer tasting and daily pint specials and a printed menu with descriptions of the up to 18 draft beers on offer at any one time. The list changes at least monthly, but typically includes: Stoudt's Abbey Ale, Saranac Golden Pilsner, Harpoon IPA, Rogue Red, and various seasonals from Brooklyn, Anchor, Sierra Nevada, Catamount and other microbreweries. In another pioneering move for a good restaurant, the draft beers are available in pitchers at fair prices.

A small front bar serves as riverrun's staging area for dining. The dining room is dominated by blond wood and has a tavern atmosphere. Suits and jeans mix easily here.

RUBY'S TAP HOUSE***

1754 Second Avenue (92nd)
212-987-8306

Serious About Beer, And Fun

Ruby's opened in late 1994 with 26 draft lines, the most in Manhattan at the time. Bravely, owners Gary Crivin and Constantine Samios gave up only two of those draft lines to the accepted, unchallenged taste of the Upper East Side: for Rolling Rock and RR Light. The other two dozen are a marvelous assemblage of good micros and imports, including:

Sierra Nevada Pale Ale, Catamount Porter, Dock Street Pilsner, Brooklyn Brown and Lager, Paulaner Hefe-Weizen, New England Oatmeal Stout, Saranac Pale Ale, Bateman's XXXB and New England Holiday Ale. Again, with emphasis, those were all on draft, and the menu changes almost daily according to what's available.

Ruby's continues to experiment on the short menu – chicken, pasta, steak, turkey, duck gumbo, for example, with sides such as bourbon yams, homemade slaw and mashed or curly-fried potatoes – and the look of the place. Muralists are plotting out wall paintings on the history of beer in America.

A good time to drop in is Wednesday around 7 p.m. when Stu and Nick, the British twins who work behind the bar, run their New York Beer Appreciation Club, with tastings, brewmaster guests, discussions and more tastings.

"We looked for a place for two years," says Crivin, a former Chumley's partner and TV sports producer. "We wanted to do the Upper East Side because there wasn't really a beer bar in the area. Our primary goal is educating people about beer and getting people in the neighborhood to be more appreciative. If someone orders a Rolling Rock, our standard offer is to buy them their next beer, whatever they want, if they try a good beer first. By the end of the night they're drinking Hefe or Oatmeal Stout." He describes the draft system as state of the art, with recirculation using a carbon dioxide and oxygen mix for regular beer, and a nitrogen mix for stouts. Hand pumps may be on the way. One other important point. Early in the evening, Ruby's welcomes kids in the small but comfortable back dining area, which includes some long tables that are great for groups.

SEVEN WILLOW STREET*

7 Willow Street, Port Chester
914-939-1474

Alternative Bands, Alternative Beers

This big old brick building is one of Westchester County's hottest spots for alternative music, drawing big crowds of people in their 20s. The beer selection changes, but there are usually some good micros. When the place isn't being used for music to mosh to, it occasionally hosts beer festivals.

SIDEWALKERS*

12 West 72nd Street (Central Park West)
212-799-6070

Dakota Country

Across the street from the celebrity-packed Dakota, the building where John Lennon lived and died, this is a large, pleasant-looking Upper West Side restaurant that does a lot of things but specializes in seafood. If you like eating crabs the right way – a big Maryland-style "crab bush" piled onto the paper-covered table right in front of you – this is the place to strap on the bib, pick up the hammer and pull up the bucket on the floor next to you. The good beer includes Duvel, Geary's, Grant's, Harpoon, New England, Rogue Old Crustacean (of course), Paulaner, Pike Place and Young's.

THE SILVER SWAN**

41 East 20th (B'way/Park)
212-254-3611

A German Secret in Gramercy

Michael Moscatt says his restaurant is "the best-kept secret in New York." When he says this, the regulars at the bar nod vigorously and murmur in assent. "But we like it that way," one mutters. "Never too hard to get a table. Or a beer." There are other places with good food and other places with good beer, yet another confides, but no place has such a good combination of the two. When Moscatt describes the atmosphere in the small (48-seat) restaurant as "like somebody's living room," the heads begin nodding again.

Moscatt runs the Silver Swan with his girlfriend, Renate Koplin, the chef responsible for a German-American menu that ranges from a liverwurst sandwich for $7 to wursts starting at $11 to roasts and sauerbraten for $15 to venison and veal chops for $25. Luckily for those of us who count beer as a vegetable when necessary to balance a meal, there is a wide choice on the Silver Swan's eight-page pamphlet headed "International Microbrewery List."

The list, which offers insightful descriptions of the beers, includes Ayinger Brau-Weisse and Jahrhundert, Paulaner Hefe-Weizen, Pike Place, Pinkus Munster Alt and Weizen, Sierra Nevada Pale Ale, and Samuel Smith's Nut Brown Ale, Oatmeal Stout, Pale Ale and Winter Welcome, MacAndrew's Scotch Ale, Lindemans Peche and Kriek, and Orval Trappist Ale.

Of special interest to those who haven't had it is Kaiserdom Rauchbier, a smoked Bavarian beer that is rare in American restaurants but would be a natural choice for barbecue joints. When Moscatt and Koplin opened their restaurant back in 1991, they couldn't decide what to name it. Moscatt wanted "The Magic Table." Koplin, however, persuaded him to use the Silver Swan image from *Lord of the Rings*.

THE SLAUGHTERED LAMB**

182 West 4th Street (6th/7th Aves)
212-627-5262

His Hair Was Perfect...

Named after the pub in the film An American Werewolf in London, this installment in the chain of Eerie Entertainment, Inc., pubs (with Jack the Ripper and the two Jekyll and Hydes) has the same strong lineup of beers as Jack's, with some but not all the special effects and tricks of the two Hydes.

There's an electrocution every so often down in the "dungeon," along with a "boiling" cauldron and a glassed-in rotating tableau of a werewolf busting out of his evening clothes as he sinks his teeth into a fair lass who is, ahem, busting out of her evening clothes, too.

Like all the Eerie Entertainment pubs, the food and beer are pricier than at the corner tavern, but the corner tavern probably doesn't have St. Sixtus Trappist Ale, Hacker-Pschorr Weisse or Samichlaus, arguably the world's strongest beer. Other standbys include Paulaner Hefe-Weizen, Corsendonk Monk's Brown Ale, Lindemans Framboise, all the Sierra Nevada brews, and English beers including Fuller's ESB, Royal Oak Pale Ale, Fuller's London Pride, and Samuel Smith's Nut Brown Ale, Oatmeal Stout, Imperial Stout and Taddy Porter.

If you haven't, and you dare, try one of the small but powerful (12 percent ABV) bottles of Thomas Hardy's Ale, a collector's beer even in its native England. Some people lay it down to age, typically for at least 10 years. "They ask when it's best," a Thomas Hardy executive said a few years back over lunch at the brewery. "I tell them it's good any time after 10...10 in the morning, that is."

For bar history buffs, the Slaughtered Lamb is on the site of the old Peculier Pub.

SOHO KITCHEN AND BAR*

103 Greene Street (Prince/Spring)
212-925-1866

A Sleek See-and-Be-Seen Scene

It's in a big old building, but there's nothing creaky or drafty about the SoHo Kitchen and Bar. It's where the young and would-be young movers and shakers who work or live in the SoHo area gather after work. These people are wearing serious suits and drinking serious beer; there's good micro and gourmet-import representation among the 30-plus bottles and on the draft lines, including Pinkus Ur Weizen, Pike Place Pale Ale, Newcastle Brown, Pete's and Sierra Nevada.

There are two different tasting flights – servings of four seven-ounce beers for a reasonable $9. The problem is that for both Flight A and Flight B, they tell you what the four beers are instead of allowing you to choose.

The paddle-shaped bar is substantial, and the small wire-backed chairs at the adjoining tables are not as uncomfortable as they look. The decor features large wooden model airplanes and goose decoys dangling among the red columns and modern art on the walls. The whole place, often noisy with the clatter so common to big Manhattan places, is a mix of old and new that somehow works. The food, according to an unscientific survey of people who have eaten there, is a reasonably-priced but undistinguished array of standards such as pizzas, burgers, steaks, salads, pasta and sandwiches.

Check out The Bureau upstairs. It's new, it's trendy, it's mockingly modeled after the FBI headquarters.

Paul Camusi and Ken Grossman began brewing in a garage. They ended up with Sierra Nevada.

STUBS*

41 Clark Street (Hicks), Brooklyn
718-834-9488

A Family/Sports Bar/Restaurant

A newish mix of brick and blond wood, this big Brooklyn Heights bar is also a family restaurant with a long tap room, a bright front dining room and a back room off the bar with tables and a giant TV screen. The food menu is extensive, including grilled salmon, pork chops, shrimp and sirloin, most of them under $15, and quite a few variations of pasta, along with a kids' menu.

There's a cooler full of micros near the bar entrance, and the draft beers include Brooklyn Lager and Samuel Adams.

TACI INTERNATIONAL*

2841 Broadway (110th)
212-678-5345

Mid-Scale Italian Uptown

Artfully designed and decorated, this restaurant-bar opened in 1993 in a good spot in the Columbia University area. The beer list reflects the way that restaurant managers are becoming more willing to try new things to remain competitive – such as a decent beer list with a mostly Italian menu. Taci's 20 beers include Chimay, Saranac, Pete's, Duvel, Sierra Nevada and Harpoon.

Anne Shapiro, the manager, says more micros and good imports may be on the way because of the positive customer response, and she's determined to expand the seasonal offerings on draft. The brickwork and mosaics inside offer a nice feel, but there's nothing like a table outside watching Broadway go by during nice weather. Few of the burgers, pasta dishes or other main courses are more than $10. The 10 bar stools and 30 tables draw a fair number of students along with professors and neighborhood people.

TASCA DO PORTO*

525 Broome Street (Thompson/Sullivan)
212-343-2321

"Tapas Not Topless"

Tasca do Porto is a funky Spanish-Portugese place where it's possible to hear five languages – English, Spanish, Portuguese, French and Swedish – in the time it takes to drink a pint of Catamount Porter. And that was early on a Tuesday evening, before the music started and the place got busy.

One flight down a metal staircase, Tasca do Porto has a good list of hot and cold tapas, mostly in the $4-6 range, along with reasonably priced dinners. Besides the Catamount on draft, there are a number of decent imported beers in bottles, along with 12 different ports, including several vintages. There's live jazz on Sunday, Monday and Tuesday nights.

"Like a camel, I can do without a drink for seven days — and have on several horrible occasions."

Herb Caen

TEDDY'S BAR**

96 Berry Street (N. 8th), Brooklyn
718-384-9787

Comforting As An Old Stuffed Toy

Updated in mood and method, this is a really good old bar that makes an admirable match with the Williamsburg section of Brooklyn – a cheerful mix of warehouses, artists' lofts and apartment dwellers from a range of ethnic groups.

Teddy's has a long wooden bar, a high tin ceiling with lazily turning fans, a tile floor, small tables with chairs and church pews. The stained glass window in front says, "Peter Doelger's Extra Beer," and dates back to the 1880s, when the bar was owned by Peter Doelger's Brewery. There's a cozy little back room (good for children) with a handful of tables and a good-sized woodburning fireplace.

There's live music almost every night, and a menu with starters, sandwiches and burgers under $5, and a blackboard with blueplate specials such as meatloaf marinara for under $10. There are a few notable beers in bottles, including Chimay Grand Reserve and Celis White, but the real attraction is the lineup of drafts, including Bass, Harp, Sierra Nevada, Harpoon, Saranac, Guinness and, of course, Brooklyn Lager. The Brooklyn Brewery warehouse, offices and new brewery tap room (ask at Teddy's or call 718-486-7422 to see if it's open yet) are a short three blocks away, on 11th just off Berry Street.

During the day the place is a nice mix of old folks, young parents with kids, resting actors, artists taking a break and people who work in the neighborhood. At night it's usually crowded and lively, but with an atmosphere that's a lot more relaxed than the intensity of the saloons across the river in Manhattan. The owners, Felice and Glenn Kirby and Lee Ornati, are unreconstructed community activists and many of the staffers are artists; all of them are friendly and welcoming. This place is worth a trip from Manhattan, particularly in combination with a visit to the Brooklyn Brewery and another good nearby bar, Mugs Alehouse.

TELEPHONE BAR AND GRILL*

149 Second Avenue (9th/10th)
212-529-5000

Your Call

The Telephone Bar is one of those places where both women and men feel comfortable sitting alone, with a good book in one hand and a good pint in the other. An especially inviting spot is the broad staircase down from the street-level entrance that features red London phone boxes inside and out.

Especially good pints, all on draft, include Bass, Newcastle Brown, Woodpecker Cider, Pilsner Urquell, Watney's Red Barrel, Fuller's ESB, Spaten Light and Amberley. The dining area adjacent the long bar serves salads, burgers, steak, fish and an appealing selection of pot pies, along with fish 'n' chips – all priced not too far on either side of $10. One of the real treats, with or without a book, is the back room with easy chairs and a fireplace.

Bert Grant, generally regarded as the world's foremost authority on hops, started the first modern-era brewpub in America, and also the first no-smoking restaurant.

TGI FRIDAY'S*

240 White Plains Road, Tarrytown
914-332-0960

And Every Other Day, Too

One of the mysteries of the restaurant and bar business is why a chain with a strong brand such as Friday's – combining food and fun, family and a good singles scene – hasn't linked its American theme and food with good American beer. So far, however, most Friday's restaurants have only dabbled in micros. This one looks like it may set a trend with Saranac Black and Tan on draft and a few other micros in bottles. This is a good Friday's that could be better with an improved selection of beer.

TRIBECA GRILL**

375 Greenwich Street (Franklin)
212-941-3900

Robert DeNiro's Class Act

You wouldn't really expect Robert DeNiro to open a restaurant where Jake LaMotta, Travis Bickle or many of his other screen personas would feel comfortable. Instead, TriBeCa Grill – DeNiro is just a partner, but customers prefer to regard the place as belonging solely to "Bobby" – is one of the best of the big, new trendy saloons in Manhattan. It was also one of the first of the really good New York restaurants to jump on the microbrew wagon.

Chef Don Pintabona's food, good but not cheap, is an admirably varied American cuisine, with lots of Mediterranean influence, and the room itself is dominated by dark green and by dark wood. Friends who haven't seen each other in a while tend to use TriBeCa Grill as the occasion for a night out, meeting at the long two-sided bar for a little cocktail party before dinner. Beverage director Michael Waterhouse changes the micros on the beer menu fairly often; on a recent visit the list included Celis White and Grant's Apple Honey Ale.

TROPICA*

MetLife Building Concourse (Grand Central)
212-867-6767

For When You're in Training

This, like the other Restaurant Associates branches in this book (American Festival Cafe and Cafe Centro's Beer Bar), is one of the city's handful of top restaurants serving good beer. Tropica, which specializes in seafood, is a good-sized and attractive restaurant that draws big lunch crowds and a respectable amount of business in the evening.

The square 30-seat bar up front offers a beer menu that includes several good micros and imports, including Brooklyn Lager, Hofbrau Pilsner and Double Diamond. There's a raw bar and conch chowder for $7, and entrees range up to $20. Train departures from Grand Central Station are shown on a screen in the bar.

A "black jack," in Olde England was a large leather bag, tarred on the outside, to carry beer.

TUBBY'S**

401 Sunrise Highway, West Islip
516-661-8976

Getting Bombed

The first thing most people notice about Tubby's, beyond the 40 tap handles sprouting behind the bar like flowers begging to be plucked, is the World War II torpedo bomb that serves as the tower supporting several draft lines. Tubby, a semi-reformed biker who maintains his nickname through a mostly liquid diet that runs through that very torpedo, tells a good story of how he looked all over the country for a bomb. Eventually, he ended up in Chinatown, and the first Chinese guy he talked to had this torpedo in back.

This bar (Tubby's Ivanhoe is his other) is a busy, unpretentious sort of place that has lots of good drinkers and lots of good beer, including a broad range of micros and imports. Some of them are: Hacker-Pschorr, Spaten, Stoudt's Honey Double Maibock, Ram Rod, Harpoon Stout, Young's Oatmeal Stout and Saranac. There are also nine television sets, two pool tables and a lot of lively conversation, from sports arguments to the good-natured, and sometimes serious-intentioned, flirting that is so much a part of so many Long Island bars.

"Teaching has ruined more American novelists than drink."

Gore Vidal

TUBBY'S IVANHOE**

661 Old Willets Path, Hauppauge
516-234-2121

The Long Island Round Table

If there's a big guy with a ponytail, a beard, a belly and a beer holding forth in front of the bar, make a point of telling him you like it. The bar, that is. That's Tubby, the owner, a former biker (Warlords, Inc., is his company) and sometime-carpenter who fashioned the bar, including the ornate carving in back, from sketches he made of the bar at the Algonquin Hotel.

It's a marvelous job of woodworking; the mahogany is oiled, not shellacked. Tubby is both, at times, while holding forth among the customers – he's rarely seen on the working side of the bar – and sampling the wares from his 24 draft lines, including Dortmunder, Paulaner, Hacker-Pschorr, Stoudt's Honey Double Maibock and Sierra Nevada Pale Ale.

The Ivanhoe, a onetime diner that still serves good food in the red leatherette booths, is located hard by the largest industrial park in the United States. One of the tenants is Reuters, the British news and information agency, so much of the after-work crowd is made up of young Brits pursuing their post-colonial right to drink strong beer, talk about soccer and complain about their American bosses. Some of the Reuters guys have a band that thrashes through its repertoire on Friday nights. All in all, a very good bar.

It is possible to drink around the clock in Berlin, where the law requires bars to close for only one hour a day.

TWINS*

1712 Second Avenue (88th/89th)
212-987-1111

Gimme A Double

One of the things that makes New York so wonderful – golly, let's go ahead and call it whacky – is the way somebody can come up with a crazy idea like having an entire restaurant staffed by twins, from the managers to the bartenders to the waitresses...and then make it come true. "Hi!" the hostesses say in stereo. From what seemed like a truly goofy idea, Twins made a remarkable start in late 1994. Yes, the first customers came for the novelty, but many of them are returning not for the novelty but for the food and drink. Which includes some Lindemans, Chimay, Samuel Smith's and good seasonals. And, yes, it's true that if you work at Twins and your twin calls in sick, you can't work, either.

Pierre Celis was a milkman before he got into brewing in his native Belgium, and then sold that brewery to start over in Austin, Tex.

VIRGIL'S REAL BARBECUE**

152 West 44th Street (6th/7th)
212-921-9494

Down Home, Times Square Style

Hush puppies and Corsendonk Pale Ale? This large (250-seat) rib joint offers the chance to experiment. Virgil's also offers a noisy, happy atmosphere that's great for kids, along with some more than passable barbecue and beers such as: Ayinger Celebrator; Anderson Valley Barney Flats Oatmeal Stout and Belk's ESB; Boon Kriek; Boont Amber; Breckenridge Amber and Avalanche, and several brews from Dock Street, Grant's and Catamount.

This is a busy place at mealtime (which can be just about any time in Manhattan), decorated with rural Americana and bar stools covered in what appears to be genuine Naugahyde-style leatherette. The hats, shirts and sauce make for good collectibles, and the $8-18 menu listings include crab cakes, biscuits, wings, po' boys, meat loaf, chops, steaks and chocolate devil's food cake. This is a "fun" place to eat but, as one review said, it might disappoint the barbecue purist. Anyone else, especially the beer purist, is going to like it a lot.

Virgil's staff undergoes a beer training program, and is well versed in advising on mixing food and beer. Be forewarned, however, about accepting the challenge of the Insanity hot sauce. You really would be crazy.

"Sometimes too much drink is barely enough."

Mark Twain

VONG**

200 East 54th Street (Third Ave)
212-486-9592

Elegant Expense-Account Thai

The beer is where it should be, on the top shelf, in the Orchid Bar at the entrance of this highly praised restaurant designed on a French colonial theme. But the bar, with its tiny chairs and delicate little tables decorated with a single orchid each, is not the sort of place most people would drop by just for a beer. Instead, this is a well-reviewed and fairly pricey restaurant popular among corporate gourmands. For lunch, appetizers begin at $10 and entrees at $20.

For those who do settle into the soothing dining room with its booths and semi-private semi-rooms in the middle, chef-owner Jean-George Vongerichten (of JoJo fame) serves up fare including several duck dishes, grilled beef in ginger broth, squab, lobster with Thai herbs, charred lamb salad and *foie gras* with ginger and mango.

Even if the waiter proffers the wine menu first, the beer list is worth asking for: Brooklyn Brown; Sierra Nevada; Anchor Steam; Duvel; Lindemans Kriek, Framboise and Peche; Samuel Smith's Nut Brown, and Castelain Ch'Ti. The latter, served in a 750ml bottle for $15, is a rare blonde Alsatian *biere de garde*, made with ale yeast but then cold-aged like lager. Hmmm, maybe Vong's Orchid Bar is a place to stop just for a beer.

Liefmans brews its beers for an entire night, an extraordinarily long time.

WATERFRONT ALE HOUSE***

136 Atlantic Avenue (Henry/Clinton), Brooklyn
718-522-3794

Peter's Place: Best of Brooklyn

It's often called Peter's Waterfront, but the owner's name is Sam Barberi, who likes to claim his bar has the best selection of beers and single malts in Brooklyn. A number of experts agree, including Michael Jackson, whose picture has pride of place on the wall from one of his visits.

The Waterfront is not a big place, but diners at the handful of tables choose from a decent menu featuring meat that has been barbecued or smoked in the back room, including a number of German preparations. The most expensive thing on the menu is grilled beer pork chops at under $15, and perhaps the best bargain is the venison and black bean chili with tequila cilantro sour cream for about $8. The lunch special, which was only $6.95 when this was written in the spring of 1995, offered the soup of the day, a choice of sandwich (hickory smoked turkey breast, baked Virginia ham, fresh roasted beef, Bavarian liverwurst, beerwurst or albacore tuna salad), cole slaw and a mug of beer.

Ah, yes, the beer. Barberi likes to call his bar "the Cheers of downtown Brooklyn," and indeed this seems like the kind of joint where Norm and Cliff could take root if they had half a chance.

There are 12 draft and 46 bottle beers, including: MacAndrews Scotch Ale; Samuel Smith's Old Brewery Pale Ale, Nut Brown Ale, Taddy Porter, Oatmeal Stout and Winter Welcome; Pike Place Pale Ale; Celebrator Doppelbock; Brasseurs; Corsendonk Pale Ale; Chimay Grand Reserve; Catamount Amber; Geary's Pale Ale; Rodenbach; Samichlaus; Thomas Hardy's Ale;

Grant's Celtic Ale and Imperial Stout; and Saison Dupont.

The wheat beer lineup is particularly strong: Ayinger Brau-Weisse and Ur-Weisse, Erdinger Dunkel Weisse and Paulaner Hefeweizen, among others. If you've never had Kwak, the 9 percent ABV, garnet-colored, licorice-wafting brew from Belgium, the Waterfront is as good a place as any. And with any smoked meat, be sure to try the Rauchbier, a Bavarian "smoked" beer made from barley malt roasted over beech-wood smoke.

WESTSIDE BREWING CO.

340 Amsterdam Avenue (76th)
212-721-2161

Upper West Side Brewpub

Westside Brewing opened a few months earlier than Yorkville, the Upper East Side brewpub, but still shares many of the cross-town competition's good and bad points. Beer weenies, as they often do, complain about the beer and the brewing process. They also complain that the Westside brewers aren't as eager as they'd like to spend time showing them around and talking to them about what the weenies think Westside Brewing is doing wrong.

Too bad for the beer weenies. Westside Brewing serves its public well, and draws the crowds to prove it. In these uptown residential areas, known for having a population thirsting for knowledge and trends, good beer and craft brewing are relatively new concepts to be discovered and embraced at certain times in life, like owning an Akita or having a baby.

Westside may not serve the most sophisticated beer around, but if it leads people to try more good gourmets and imports, or to educate themselves about what makes a good beer taste good, then who's to knock it? A former J.G. Melon's that was a hangout for the first young upwardly mobiles back in the early 1980s, this very bar is where one of the then-regulars, the journalist Jane See White, over an Amaretto coined the term "YP's" for young professionals, which quickly evolved into the full Y-word.

The food includes a full menu of pub grub, snacks, steaks, fish and pasta. The variety of beers are familiar for any new brewpub: the Blonde, the Wheat, the Red, the Nut Brown and several fruit variations.

WHITE HORSE TAVERN

567 Hudson Tavern (11th)
212-243-9260

Drinking With A Literary Ghost

The White Horse Tavern is an old, worn, comfortable and otherwise undistinguished tavern that seems to do much of its business because of its Dylan Thomas connection. Thomas, the Welshman whose reputation as a poet was surpassed only by his reputation as a drunk, died in 1953 in New York at age 39 of alcohol abuse.

One of his favorite Manhattan haunts was the White Horse, where he supposedly had his last fling. According to the much-debated story, he staggered back to the apartment where he was staying, and announced that he had just consumed 19 straight whiskies. "I believe that's a record," he reputedly declared. He then collapsed for his own not-so-gentle journey into that good night.

Unfortunately, the White Horse today doesn't have much beer as interesting as some of the Thomas stuff on the walls. The house ale, made by New Amsterdam, is the best on tap. The owner, incidentally, is named Jim Munson but is not to be confused with the Jim Munson of Brooklyn who does beer lectures and oversees gourmet-beer tastings.

YORKVILLE BREWERY

1359 First Avenue (73rd)
212-517-2739

Upper East Side Brewpub

A very welcome addition to the neighborhood when it opened in October 1994, the Yorkville Brewery quickly became and has remained a popular dining and drinking spot. The relatively few homebrewers and beer nerds who wander in are less than universally appreciative of the beer. "It's like they decided to brew Bud, Killian's and Sam Adams," one beer weenie groans.

But that's not the point. Yorkville Brewery is serving a customer base that regards a brewpub as a new and exciting concept – people who are perhaps just discovering beer and its many possibilities. In time, Yorkville Brewery may be forced to craft more challenging beers, or beers that meet the inevitable demands of its customers for something different, darker, stronger, spicier. There are already signs that the brewery is getting bolder with its efforts to make a Porter, a Holiday Spice Ale and other new brews.

The place itself is large and sleek, all wood and copper and bronze, with plenty of room for sitting or standing at the bar, and some big booths and tables for group dining or drinking. The food includes pizza, burgers, soups, salads, pasta and entrees such as pork chops with apple sauce and beer-battered shrimp. Ask for the beer menu and the description of Yorkville's brewing process.

The brewtanks hold pride of place in the front window, while the fermenters are in the back and the cold storage and dispensing tanks are in the basement.

Young's still delivers kegs to some London pubs by horsedrawn carts.

ZIP CITY

3 W. 18th Street (Fifth Ave)
212-366-6333

The Pilsner Brewing Palace

Zip City is a big place in the Flatiron District, with a real brewery feel to the high ceilings, great aroma of hops, long horseshoe bar and, of course, the brewing works. The brewing equipment itself, one of the most expensive and most high-tech brewpub systems anywhere in America, allows Zip to make lighter, German-style lagers more easily than many other brewpubs with less advanced equipment.

Two or three of these Zip brews are generally on draft at any time: Helles, a malty Munich pale golden; Pilsner, heavily hopped with Czech Saaz hops, a double decoction mash; Weisse, a Bavarian-style wheat; Vienna, a malty amber; Märzen, a deep amber; Dunkel, a mild dark; Bock, a strong lager, and a number of seasonals and specials such as the Oktoberfest, the Doppelbock and the Rauchbier.

Zip City's bar menu has some nice touches, such as the Dagwood hero, the pulled pork barbecue sandwich, the tuna chili and the honey-roast turkey Reuben, all for around $10. Peel-and-eat shrimp, clams and oysters are also a specialty.

Zip City is also the leader among New York brewpubs in beer events, including dinners and tastings. Tours are given on weekend afternoons at 2 p.m., on Tuesdays at 7 p.m. and by special appointment.

The name, incidentally, comes from novelist Sinclair Lewis. His most famous character, George F. Babbitt, spoke glowingly of the "zip" among the citizens of the mythical city of Zenith, and called it "Zip City" (page 152 of the Signet Classic version of *Babbitt*) in a boosterism speech at the local real estate board's dinner. Zip City's logo is a little man (ol' G.F. Babbitt?) jumping through a hoop. Nice.

ZÖE*

90 Prince Street (Mercer/Broadway)
212-966-6722

One of the Best-Reviewed
Restaurants in Soho

An overnight Soho landmark, Zöe is a so-called "destination" for people from other parts of the city. It continues to be widely and positively reviewed for its eclectic American nouveau menu. Food is prepared and then served from the variety of wood-fired ovens and grills in the open kitchen at the back of the dining room. The dining room's big pinkish columns sound garish but actually look good. There's a small bar at the entrance with a modest but thoughtful beer menu designed to complement the food, including Brooklyn Brown and offerings from both Catamount and New York Harbor.

STORES:

The Best Groceries, Supermarkets, Deli's and Beverage Centers

---

Supermarket Chains

The following supermarket chains, which have dozens of branches in and around New York, are not beer specialists, but all have beverage departments that feature good American micro-brews and gourmet imports. Look in the telephone book or ask around for the stores and locations near you.

D'Agostino

Food Emporium

Gristede

Associated Supemarkets

Sloan's

Pioneeer

Red Apple

Manhattan Stores

B&E BEVERAGE

511 W. 23rd Street (10th/11th)
212-243-6559

This mini-warehouse is perhaps the closest Manhattan offers to a big suburban beverage center. The neighborhood isn't the greatest (no, B&E doesn't stand for breaking and entering), but there's semi-legal parking in front, very good prices and cases stacked high. There's also an outstanding array of big bottles from Belgium, England, France and various American micro-breweries. The staff is friendly, helpful and knowledgeable. Ask for Benny or his wife Elky, who have vowed to carry every good beer they can get, or their main man Marco, who loves to recommend beers and talk about the good life back in his native Puerto Rico. This is the place to go to stock up for big parties.

BROADWAY FARM

2339 Broadway (85th)
212-787-8585

This is a staple place, and a place for staples, on the Upper West Side. It's large and jammed with the fresh and fragrant, but non-Manhattan residents should be forewarned: the prices may cause sticker shock. There are a lot of single bottle sales, but more six-packs than in the smaller neighborhood deli's. There are a few displays of cases, including some special prices.

FANCY GROCERY

329 Bleecker Street (Christopher)
212-929-6546

It ain't fancy, and it ain't really a grocery, but it is the best little beer house in the West Village. From this remarkably tiny store, which also offers cat food, ice cream, toilet paper, sticks of firewood and a few other things people need late at night, an incredible amount of the best beer in the world is sold. Fittingly for Village people, it's sold by one of the best-known characters in a neighborhood full of folks who would be the craziest characters in almost any other neighborhood in America. His name is Hercules Dimitratos, and he'd be very happy to talk beer with you.

Brusque, charming, distracted, doting, Hercules may be different things to different people. But he knows his beer, and is known for fighting with distributors to get the first, the best and the most of whatever his customers want. He's there at 3 in the afternoon, he's there at 3 in the morning, and he has a mantra when asked about his many gourmet imports and micros: "Yeah, dat's good beer." And he's right.

INDIA SPICE HOUSE

99 First Avenue (6th)
212-387-7812

Need an extension cord? A ruler? Drano? A 25-pound bag of rice? Curry, paprika, coriander or any of dozens more spices? Good beer? Try the Spice House. If you're eating at one of the neighborhood restaurants without a liquor license, stop here first to pick up your beer and get in the mood with the amazing smells. A very sensual place, sniff-wise and beer-wise, and a true challenge to people who think they can identify or distinguish different smells all mingled together.

MAMA JOY'S DELI

2892 Broadway (112th/113th)
212-662-8122

This is a great old inner-city grocery, with a busy deli counter. There's a good but not huge selection of beer, including some things not usually seen on grocery shelves, such as Samichlaus and Samuel Adams Triple Bock. Herb, who runs Mama's, has been a real beer pioneer on the Upper West Side, and anything that he and his staff don't have, they'll order for you.

VILLAGE FARM GROCERY

146 Second Avenue (9th/10th)
212-475-7521

The Village Farm is indicative of the reasons there are so many good, inexpensive ethnic places to dine in the East Village. It's geared toward its customers, people who generally watch their money and live in small places. They haven't the cash, the storage space or the inclination to stockpile. Its European feel is underscored by the good selection of beer, much of it sold in single bottles to people who take them into the good, inexpensive neighborhood ethnic restaurants that don't have liquor licenses.

VILLAGE BAZAAR

124 Second Avenue (7th/8th)
212-460-9608

Just by standing in front of the Village Bazaar, these ethnic restaurants are in sight: Thai, Vietnamese, Israeli, Yemeni, Indian, Ukrainian. The United Nations role call continues up and down the avenue and around the corner of every side street. Inside the tiny store, the necessities of life are for sale: aspirin, toilet paper and beers to go quite nicely with the food served in all those restaurants, many of which don't have liquor licenses. Odds are you'll stand on line with someone you see later at the next table. One of the life-changing revelations of the 1990s has been how well a good strong American micro-brew goes with spicy food from halfway around the world.

WEST WAY FOODS

375 Amsterdam Avenue (78th)
212-724-2322

This is one of those groceries catering to the Upper West Side lifestyle that includes a fridge stocked with little more than yogurt and mineral water – and a lot of eating out. West Way is a real supermarket in the same way that Pop Tarts is real food. Fortunately, part of the lifestyle includes good beer now and then, and West Way has a lot of that, including some good hard-to-find brands.

The Best of the Rest in Manhattan

Alex's Deli
95 Macdougal Street
212-979-7826

Apple Tree Deli
1225 Amsterdam Avenue
212-865-8840

Columbia Deli Center
64 Tiemann Place
212-865-9523

D & H Gourmet Deli
540 Amsterdam Avenue
212-875-0245

Dean & Deluca
560 Broadway (Crosby)
212-431-1691

East Village Farm
69 Second Avenue
212-477-1385

Grill Beverage
350 West Street
212-463-7171

Houston Beer
298 E. 2nd Street
212-677-1460

New Cathedral Fruit Market
2853 Broadway
212-678-6213

Schact's Deli
99 Second Avenue
212-420-8219

S.O.K. Market
100 Avenue A
212-777-8660

West Side Market
2844 Broadway (110th/111th)

University Food Market
2941-49 Broadway
212-666-4190

Brooklyn, Queens Stores

AMERICAN THRIFTY BEVERAGE

252 Court Street (Kane), Brooklyn
718-875-0226

Many in the beer business regard this Carroll Gardens landmark as perhaps the best beer store in all of New York City. It's large, bright, clean, well-organized and well-run by Janet and Joe Marino, brother and sister whose grandfather and father ran the business before them. There's plenty of help, knowledgeable in English, Spanish and beerspeak in both languages.

"We've worked really hard to make this place nice," Joe says. "It's almost like a wine shop."

While Joe handles much of the backroom grunt work, Janet is responsible for the retail space, which shows her marketing education at Boston College is being put to good use, from the well-planned displays of big bottles and hard-to-find beers to the collection of hats, glasses and T-shirts for sale.

"My brother laughs about me making it into a ladies' beer shop," Janet says, grinning, "but in fact this is a place where we get a lot of women. Men or women, we get a discerning customer, an experienced beer drinker who's probably well-traveled. We don't get many guys running in and grabbing a case of Bud and running out. Our customers often come in and spend 20-30 minutes looking around."

American Thrifty, the only beer store to advertise in the *New York Times*, draws many customers from Manhattan and even outside the city, but the backbone of the business is still the locals. "It's not unusual for somebody to come in and say they're having a dinner party, what beers should they serve?" Janet says. "We help them out, down to asking about the people who are coming to the party. Right now people want service, and either you give them good service or they go somewhere else. Service and fresh beer, that's our emphasis. You can go to a deli that's well stocked, but you don't know how fresh it is."

BEER BARREL DISTRIBUTORS

169-05 26th Avenue, Queens
718-352-1111

Mike Rosen, who ran a watch business, and his buddy Marty Schulman, a computer consultant, decided to open this shop in 1994 in order to "recession-proof" themselves. Perhaps because neither had any experience in the beer business, they have been extraordinarily receptive to the idea of stocking new and different beers.

Their whole store in Flushing is geared toward micros and imports, and they boast of having beer that is available nowhere else in New York State – some of which their respective daughters bring back from their out-of-state colleges. When people come in and try to buy something mundane, Mike and Marty say, "Hey, right, for $4.50 you can have a six of that and pound it down just like everyone else. For a couple of bucks more you can be an individual; you can try a good beer and have a couple of them now and a couple of them later." Indeed, their newspaper ads promote all their gourmet brews but then admit, in small print at the bottom, "We Also Sell Bud."

Customers looking for a brand they had on vacation or heard about, Mike and Marty bend over backwards to get it for them. Ever had Red Ass Ale from Fort Collins? Nantucket? Mill City? Boston Burton? Door County Golden Rail? St. Andrews? Mike and Marty will not only sell you those, they'll let you mix them in a six-pack with each bottle priced at the six-pack price instead of the higher per-bottle price.

COBBLE HEIGHTS BEER

216 Pacific Street (Court), Brooklyn
718-596-0871

Tom Daly, the owner, has maintained a warehouse feel for this combination wholesale-retail operation. Shoppers come in through the big front door, wander back among the pallets of cases and kegs, and then take their purchases to the window up front. Daly deals in volume, but also knows how to take care of the discerning customer and is himself very up on good micros and imports.

He tells of one customer who came in raving about Red Dog. "Why is that good beer?" asked Daly, who had obviously tasted the Miller product himself. "Because I had it in a bar for $1 a bottle," the guy answered. You can lead 'em to good beer, Daly reckoned, but there are still some who won't drink it.

KEY FOOD

169 Atlantic Avenue (Clinton), Brooklyn
718-625-2253

Quite a few Key supermarkets and groceries carry a good selection of gourmet beer, but the choice at this store is certainly among the broadest at any supermarket in all of New York City. Look for seasonal specials with food tie-ins, including sale prices on featured beer stacked at the front of aisles.

LASSEN & HENNIG

114 Montague Street (Henry/Hicks),
Brooklyn
718-522-5464

This is perhaps Brooklyn Heights' best gourmet deli. It's a small place, but packed with good quality and hard-to-find provisions. Among the necessities for civilized life in the big city are the many beers in the cooler at the back. To help guide and educate the consumer, there's a beer booklet on a string attached to the cooler doors. More places large and small should make this kind of information available.

PEAS 'N' PICKLES

79 Henry Street (Pineapple), Brooklyn
718-596-8219

This is a good deli-grocery in the Heights, with a nice selection of American micros and frequent displays and specials for quality imports. If they don't have it, ask. They'll get it if they can.

RUSSIN THRIFTY BEVERAGE

402-412 Meeker Avenue (Manhattan),
Brooklyn
718-383-2200

In the shadow of the Brooklyn-Queens Expressway, this tidy store with red-and-white floor tiles offers the best selection of beer in Williamsburg. Just go to the cases of Pabst Blue Ribbon for $7.99 and take a left towards the micro/import alcove, which has a nice selection of both, including a variety of Polish beers.

SUPER ACE SUPERMARKET

75 7th Avenue (Berkeley), Brooklyn
718-783-3806

This is a real old-fashioned working-class neighborhood grocery store, down to the worn wooden plank floors. There's nothing out of date about the beer selection, however, including a nice array of Belgians and American micros.

The Best of the Rest in Brooklyn/Queens

Apple Tree Deli
170 Seventh Avenue, Brooklyn
718-768-4691

Beer Company
686 Fourth Avenue, Brooklyn
718-499-9133

Bellrose Thrifty
240-09 Jamaica Avenue, Bellrose
718-343-0870

Community Beverage
80-04 Grand Avenue, Elmhurst
718-458-5254

Culver Narrows Thrifty
990 MacDonald Avenue, Brooklyn
718-854-6156

International Taste
150 Seventh Avenue, Brooklyn
718-768-7217

P & C Beverage
500 Fourth Avenue, Brooklyn
718-768-4455

Tai's Gourmet Food
154 Seventh Avenue, Brooklyn
718-788-4971

Two Kims
79 Seventh Avenue, Brooklyn

Long Island Stores

BEVERAGE CENTRAL

724 Montauk Highway, Bayport
516-472-9808

This place was set up by Harry Miller alongside his pool hall and rare coin shop, and all three are among the biggest of their kind on Long Island. In the beverage center, two of the 80-foot aisles are devoted to micros and two more to imports. The big walk-in cold box, larger than some entire beer stores, is accessed through a couple of dozen cooler doors, allowing for a much wider selection of already-cold beer than most places have. The American microbrews here, including quite a few that are often hard to find, are arranged in alphabetical order instead of by state or region.

BIG Z BEVERAGE BARN

1675 E. Jericho Turnpike, Huntington
516-499-3479

It's a good thing for Long Island beer drinkers that Tony Zawadzki wasn't just a little bit better football player. If so, he would have stuck with one of those NFL teams instead of using the money he saved from various tryout camps to get into the beer business.

His store, Big Z, is one of the best anywhere in New York, and it's getting better. He boasts the largest beer selection in the state – 612 at last count. "Including a lot of obscure beers," he says. The total is going up as fast as he can find new micros and imports. Zawadzki goes out of his way to serve his sophisticated customers and educate the unsophisticated. His monthly newsletter, for example, describes different styles of beer, different brands he carries, new arrivals, seasonals, specials, sales, etc. If he gets a new beer, he describes its taste, details of the brewing process and something about the brewers. (Even if you won't ever shop here, get on the mailing list.)

"The American public is getting attuned," he says. "They're not buying TV ads any more. They're buying good beer and drinking a couple of them. People are health conscious and quality conscious."

Zawadzki credits Mike Vitale, who runs the Craft Brewers Guild's operations on Long Island, for introducing him to micros and imports, but he and his staff deserve the credit for aggressively promoting good beer and making this one of the best and most service-oriented stores in the entire Northeast.

FRANK'S BEER & SODA

54 Cedar Swamp Road, Glen Cove
516-676-4126

Frank's was one of the first beverage centers on Long Island to get into micros and gourmet imports, and the two new owners, Joseph Gulino and Mario Bencivenni, are carrying on the tradition. Many of the micros are displayed in a pair of pleasant wooden alcoves, apart from the cardboard stacks of commercial stuff. There are eight-bottle samples of American micros and "Beers of the World," and a mix-and-match rack.

A regular feature is the micro of the month, typically offered at the same price as a big brand name from one of the large breweries. "We get people to try it, and pretty soon they're off the corporate beer for good," Gulino says.

LIBERTY BEVERAGE BARN

2080 Front Street, East Meadow
516-794-4818

Henry Kane, the owner, loves Chimay, and it shows. He also believes in bringing good micros to people at reasonable prices, and that shows, too. On one recent visit, he was selling New York Harbor, Saranac and Brooklyn Lager for $4.99 per six-pack, and Brooklyn for $17.95 per case. Harpoon Winter Warmer was a mere $6.99 for a six, and three bottles of Samuel Smith's were $8.99. A good place for bargains.

MONARCH BEVERAGE BARN

505 Long Beach Road, Long Beach
516-432-6615

To say this is one of the best beer stores on the south shore of Long Island is to make unfair geographic limitations. Monarch has a terrific selection, and it's getting better. "Any distributor knows that any new gourmet beer they get, they should automatically send us five cases," says co-owner Barry Levinsohn.

Monarch makes up its own gift packs – the New York Sampler, the American Micro Sampler, the English, Belgian, etc., samplers – and will ship them anywhere it's legal in the United States. Write, phone or fax (516-432-5249) for their Gourmet Beer Catalog, which includes a "Beer 101" feature explaining different beers and brewing styles.

People who come in and buy two six-packs of micro beer are usually rewarded with a free bottle from some other micro they've never tried. "And if you call us and ask us if we can get you some hard-to-find beer, we'll call you back and let you know even if we weren't able to get it," Levinsohn says.

VILLAGE BEVERAGE

202 Main Street, Setauket
516-751-8464

This is a good Long Island shop where the owners, brothers Jim and Doug Burns, stock a
respectable list of good beer. Like all good beer
sellers, they encourage customers to ask for anything they don't see. If at all possible, they'll get
it in as soon as they can.

Best of the Rest on Long Island

All Island Beverage
2776 Merrick Road, Bellmore
516-679-2800

Bayshore Beverage Barn
5th Avenue and Garfield, Bayshore
516-665-0320

Beer City
1371 Deer Park Avenue, North Babylon
516-242-1120

Bluebell Beer
8 Gates Avenue, Greenlawn
516-261-9100

C & N Beverage
4236 Hicksville Road, Bethpage
516-579-7416

County Line Enterprises
5840 Merrick Road, Massapequa
516-541-1199

Demar Beverage
371 Route 25A, Northport
516-757-7150

East Northport Beverage
306 Larkfield Road, Northport
516-368-9440

Ferro Beverage Thrifty
2280 Jericho Turnpike, Garden City Park
516-742-0114

Forest Pork Store
*380 East Jericho Turnpike, Huntington
Station*
516-423-2574

Hauppauge Beverageland
1745 Expressway Drive North, Hauppauge
516-348-7632

Isemway Beverage
279 New York Avenue, Huntington
516-427-8488

Lake Ronkonkoma Beverage
316 Smithtown Road, Lake Ronkonkoma
516-588-3320

Little Neck Beverage Barn
6 Middle Neck Road, Roslyn
516-365-1280

Lynbrook USA Beverage World
79 Sunrise Highway, Lynbrook
516-887-7658

Massapequa Park Thrifty
8 Harbor Lane, Massapequa Park
516-541-2646

Peconic Beverage
199 Pantigo Road, East Hampton
516-324-0602

Peconic Beverage
74 North Highway, South Hampton
516-537-1644

Port Washington Beer
152 Shore Road, Port Washington
516-767-0810

Rocky Point Distributors
650 Route 25A, Rocky Point
516-744-2566

Rogia Beverage
623 Sunrise Highway, West Babylon
516-587-5004

Seaford Thrifty Beverage Fair
3600 Merrick Road, Seaford
516-785-2920

South Bay Beverage
4165 Merrick Road, South Massapequa
516-798-9530

Sparkling Beverage
260 Old Country Road, Hicksville
516-942-0490

Stony Brook Beverage Corp.
710 Route 25A, Setauket
516-941-4545

Suffolk Beer
510 E. Main Street, Patchogue
516-475-0480

Syosset Beverage
600 Jericho Turnpike, Syosset
516-496-7271

Valley Stream Beverage
114 Franklyn Avenue, Valley Stream
516-568-2954

Williston Park Beverage Barn
396 Willis Avenue, Mineola
516-746-0231

Westchester, Rockland Stores

KATONAH BEVERAGE BARN

24 Woodbridge Road, Katonah
914-232-7842

Katonah Beverage Barn could be a model for any beer store in an upscale suburban area. Crammed into an old house, the inventory turns over rapidly – which in turns guarantees fresh supplies. The three partners, John Murray, Bob Stover and Sandy Bueti, have made a real point of serving their customers, whether making up microbrew giftpacks or offering advice on beer for different courses for dinner parties or scoring glassware for folks who truly believe Duvel tastes better out of a Duvel glass.

They maintain a beer library, including videos of Michael Jackson's "The Beer Hunter" television series, which they loan to customers. They arrange tastings in local restaurants every month or so, and they offer discount prices for people who want to have tastings of their own. In areas like Westchester where there are people who want good beer and are willing to pay for it, Katonah Beverage's standards of selection and service have built them an extremely loyal and increasingly adventurous following.

ROUTE 59 BEVERAGE DISCOUNT

388 Route 59 West (W. of Route 303),
West Nyack
914-358-8115

Phil Bosco started this busy center, but now concentrates on the nearby party center, Balloons 'N' Stuff, while his daughter Paula runs the beer business. Route 59 has that great smell of cardboard and beer, of cases and bottles waiting to be cracked. It also has Paula, who loves to talk beer.

"Hey, I'm a beer drinker myself," Paula says, seating herself on a stack of cases of Cave Creek Chili Beer. "Bud, Coors and Miller are not a factor in our business." Indeed, when she rearranges her shop, it's to put the Big Three farther in the back, in yet a smaller corner, so she can expand the micros and imports and leave her customers more room to browse. "We even get people coming over from New Jersey, who have to pay the deposit over here, because of our selection," she says.

RYE BEVERAGE CENTER

Boston Post Road, Rye
914-967-6088

Walk in the front door and you run smack into the Mix-A-Micro shelf, which invites customers to make up their own six-packs and cases at the six-pack or case price, instead of the higher per-bottle price. "People get hooked on 'em," says owner Jim Kelly. "It's like anything that's good quality. Once you've got 'em, they can't go back."

YORKTOWN BEER AND SODA

1893 Commerce Street, Yorktown Heights
914-962-4659

This bright store isn't all that huge but has a nice selection, including a long wall of micros and imports just beyond the impressive stack of seasonals right inside the door. "My customers got me started on micros, but now I'm way ahead of them," Glenn Cinelli, the manager, says. "People are buying less beer, but it's better beer. They want quality." The prices are good, and include occasional specials on microbrews for $1 (or less) per bottle.

The Best of the Rest in Westchester, Rockland Counties

Bavarian Beverage
645 Saw Mill River Road, Ardsley
914-693-3339

Brewster Beer & Soda
Route 22, Brewster
914-279-7094

Cable Beverage
305 Route 304, Bardonia
914-623-7645

County Beverage
28 Webster Avenue, New Rochelle
914-636-7616

Fiore Beverage
205 South Highland Avenue, Ossining
914-941-1234

Harrison Beverage Center
53 Halstead Avenue, Harrison
914-835-4741

Montrose Beer & Soda
505 Albany Post Road, Crugers
914-739-2211

Vista Market
Route 123, South Salem
914-533-6627

STAY IN TOUCH

The Craft Brewers Guild, formed to promote the dozens of quality American microbrews and gourmet imported beers distributed by the Brooklyn Brewery, would like to hear what you think of this book, both in general and regarding specific entries. If there are places that should be added, dropped or evaluated differently, please let us know why. We welcome your opinions.

Also, we'd welcome your name on the mailing list for our newsletter on beer news and events in and around New York.

The Craft Brewers Guild
118 N. 11th Street
Brooklyn NY 11211

Fax: 718-486-7440

E-mail: BeerGuild@aol.com

Incidentally, the Craft Brewers Guild logo is designer Milton Glaser's interpretation of a drinking lion depicted on an artifact from the ancient Sumerian city of Ur. The symbol of the Lion of Ur was found among other archeological evidence of breweries dating from the very dawn of civilization.